More of it's so NATURAL

Alan Hayes

📖 Angus&Robertson
An imprint of HarperCollins*Publishers*

Angus&Robertson
An imprint of HarperCollins*Publishers,* Australia

First published in Australia in 1995
Reprinted in 1996 by
HarperCollins*Publishers* Pty Limited
ACN 009 913 517
A member of the HarperCollins*Publishers* (Australia) Pty Limited Group

HarperCollins*Publishers*
25 Ryde Road, Pymble, Sydney, NSW 2073, Australia
31 View Road, Glenfield, Auckland 10, New Zealand
77-85 Fulham Palace Road, London W6 8JB, United Kingdom
Hazelton Lanes, 55 Avenue Road, Suite 2900, Toronto, Ontario M5R 3L2
and 1995 Markham Road, Scarborough, Ontario M1B 5M8, Canada
10 East 53rd Street, New York NY 10032, USA

National Library of Australia Cataloguing-in-Publication data:

Hayes, Alan B. (Alan Bruce), 1949 –
More of it's so natural.
ISBN 0 207 18823 8.
1. Home economics. 2. Herbs.
3. Environmental protection I. Title.
640.41

Printed in Hong Kong

9 8 7 6 5 4 3 2   96 97 98 99

For all those people who care

FOREWORD

Because of the pressures of modern living, many people adopt a quick-fix approach, relying on whatever's readily available at the local supermarket. However an instant panacea usually isn't the most desirable solution, and for virtually all chores around the home there's a simple, natural alternative.

In past centuries the human race always turned to nature — to the plants and earth — to make medicines, cosmetics, soaps and other beneficial products. Our great-grandparents were well aware of the many advantages these natural products possessed and made them using skills passed down from previous generations. Sadly, much of their knowledge has been gradually lost by newer generations. But it can be rediscovered.

We can learn these simple skills, which are just as effective today as they were for our ancestors, and also provide a worthwhile and interesting hobby.

More of It's So Natural shows you many environmentally sound practices for the home. It tells you how to make safe, natural products for washing, cleaning and a myriad of other household needs. There are dozens and dozens of solutions and suggestions, based on my highly successful and popular *It's So Natural* newspaper columns, that will enable you to save money and work in harmony with the environment.

Alan B. Hayes

ABRASIONS

See Cuts and Abrasions, and Tea Tree Oil.

ACHING FEET

See Foot Care.

ACHING JOINTS AND MUSCLES

Add half a cup of bicarbonate soda to a comfortably hot bath and enjoy a long, relaxing soak.

ALLERGIES

See Hay Fever.

ANIMAL FIRST AID

ABSCESS

If it has burst, cut away the hair from around the wound and bathe gently with warm salt water until the area is thoroughly clean. Once the pus has discharged, apply 1 drop of lavender oil.

CUTS, GRAZES, BITES AND SCRATCHES

Add 2 drops of thyme oil to warm salt water and wash the area carefully with this solution to prevent infection, then apply 1 drop of undiluted lavender oil.

ECZEMA AND MANGE

See Tea Tree Oil.

RHEUMATISM

Often a problem in older animals, rheumatism can cause considerable discomfort. To help ease the animal's pain, dilute 5 drops of camomile oil, 5 drops of ginger oil and 2 drops of rosemary oil in 30 ml of olive oil and massage well into the affected

area. Store any excess made-up blend in an airtight, amber-coloured glass bottle until it is needed again.

RINGWORM
Apply undiluted cider vinegar to the sores six times each day. (Don't forget that ringworm is caused by a fungus and is easily transmitted to children from cats and dogs, and then from child to child, so keep children away from pets until ringworm has cleared.)

SKIN PROBLEMS
Application of the following lotion will help to ease rashes and other skin problems.

10 ml evening primrose oil
5 drops lavender oil
5 drops camomile oil
30 ml olive oil

Thoroughly blend all the oils and store in an airtight, amber-coloured glass bottle. Apply as required to affected areas.

SORES
Treat promptly by cleaning with a warm salt and water solution and applying 1 drop of undiluted lavender oil to prevent the development of infection.

ANIMAL HEALTH
For a relatively small monetary outlay, people receive untold benefits from their pets. Correct care will ensure your pet's health and wellbeing.

KEEPING PETS CLEAN
Clean and dry bedding for furry friends and cage hygiene for the feathered variety will ensure that parasites (like lice and the mites that cause mange) and bacterial problems are nipped in the bud. Both animal bedding and bird cages should be regularly and thoroughly scrubbed using hot soapy water followed by a hot salty water rinse, then allowed to dry in the sun. Don't forget to clean food and water containers as well, and the pet itself.

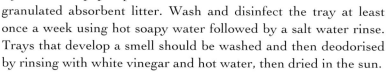

Dogs and cats can be dry washed using bicarbonate of soda to deodorise and cleanse the fur and remove excess oil when a water bath is impractical. Sprinkle the bicarbonate soda through the animal's fur then brush out well with a soft-bristle brush kept especially for this purpose.

Pets' litter trays should have a thick layer of newspaper placed underneath granulated absorbent litter. Wash and disinfect the tray at least once a week using hot soapy water followed by a salt water rinse. Trays that develop a smell should be washed and then deodorised by rinsing with white vinegar and hot water, then dried in the sun.

Birds' perches should be removed at least once every month and scrubbed with warm water and pure soap. Rinse in salty water and allow to dry in the sun. Likewise, scour aviary nesting boxes using salt and hot water, then sun-dry.

ANIMAL INDISCRETIONS

Dogs and cats are loved and pampered by human beings, treated like members of the family and provide loving companionship, loyal devotion and, in some circumstances, act as stalwart defenders. However, no matter how much we see our pet as one of the family, there are times when some of their qualities and not so pleasant habits cause problems.

DOG WASH

See Eucalyptus Oil and separate Dog Wash entry.

EXCRETA AND VOMIT

Remove as much of the excreta or vomit from the carpet as you can using a

spatula or piece of cardboard, being careful not to push any solid matter into the pile. Mop up any moisture with an old cloth. Blend together 2 cups of soap flakes, half a cup of methylated spirits and 30 ml of eucalyptus oil, then dissolve 2 tablespoons of this mixture in 4 litres of warm water. Saturate a cloth in this solution and sponge the dirty area with the rung-out cloth. Store the remaining undiluted mixture in an airtight glass jar. This mixture can also be used for hand-washing woollens.

URINE STAINS

Urine stains can be removed using the same eucalyptus mixture. To eliminate any after-odour, add 12 drops of lavender oil to a cup of bicarbonate of soda, mixing well with your hands. Sprinkle this powder over the affected spot using a flour sifter, leave for 2 hours and vacuum up.

FLEAS

Essential oils are an excellent natural choice for controlling fleas and other parasites on your pets because they don't disturb the skin and coat's natural oil balance.

If you shampoo your pet weekly you can discourage fleas and other parasites by adding 1 drop of lemongrass or citronella oil to the shampoo. Use 2 drops for large dogs, like Great Danes.

Cats can be treated for fleas and parasites by adding 1 drop of pennyroyal oil to the tip of the tail and then working it up through the fur of the body. Do not apply more than a drop, because pennyroyal is a powerful essential oil that can be dangerous to cats in larger amounts.

Brushing the animal with cedarwood or pine lotion will disinfect and condition the coat and collect any parasites and their eggs lurking within. Secure a piece of thick flannel material over the teeth of a steel brush. Add 4 drops of cedarwood or pine oil to a bowl of warm water and soak the covered brush in this lotion before using it to brush your pet's coat. Rinse the brush in the lotion repeatedly while brushing.

If the animal is suffering from a very serious flea infestation, add 4 drops of cedarwood oil directly to the piece of material. Rub well to disperse the oil before securing to the brush and use plain water for rinsing several times while brushing.

Treating the animal will be a waste of time if you don't attend to the living areas it frequents as well. All sleeping areas and bedding should be kept dry and treated with an appropriate repellent. Herbs such as dried pennyroyal, cedarwood shavings or pine needles can be scattered on and underneath bedding, or make a large pillow stuffed with insect-repelling herbs for your pet to sleep on. Include the previous three, or stinking roger, wormwood, tansy or native peppermint.

See also Dog Wash, Eucalyptus Oil and Flea Repellents.

FLIES

See Eucalyptus Oil.

TERRITORIAL CLAIMS

Thoroughly wash down animal 'claims' around doorways using warm soapy water, then disinfect the area with a solution of 20 drops of lavender oil in 10 ml of methylated spirits blended with a litre of tepid water. This solution should be used immediately.

Animal urine and faeces in garden beds smell bad — and they'll probably kill your favourite plants as well. A simple solution is to plant *Solenostemon canis* throughout the garden in amongst your other plants. This small perennial can be used for border planting and is a very effective repellent to both dogs and cats. You will, however, need to plant it in clean or sterilised soil because it won't be effective if the area already smells strongly of the scent of the animal who has made a claim.

If the cat nextdoor uses your garden as its toilet, plant *Solenostemon canis* and discuss the problem with your neighbours. Encourage them to plant the herb *Nepeta cataria* (better known as catnip) around their garden. Cats love it, will roll on it and even eat it, and will be very happy animals.

The *Solenostemon* will deter an unwanted cat from your yard and the catnip will ensure it stays where it belongs.

Deterrent Spray

This will also help to keep cats from staking their claims in and around your yard and garden.

Grind up a whole bulb of garlic and mix with 1 teaspoon of cayenne pepper and 1 litre of tepid water. Cover, steep for two hours, then strain through muslin cloth into a suitable watering can or plastic pump-spray bottle. Use whenever necessary.

ANISE

Aniseed oil is reputed to relieve sinusitis and related problems. Simply put 3 drops of oil on the back of the tongue.

Many fishing enthusiasts also use aniseed oil as a lure for fish, rubbing it well into their hands before baiting their hooks. Try it next time you go fishing – many successful anglers swear by it.

ANT BITE

See Stings and Bites.

APPETITE

A cup of caraway tea, drunk half an hour before a meal or whenever desired, acts as a powerful, natural appetite stimulant. Infuse 1 tea-spoon of crushed, dried seeds in a ceramic cup for five minutes. Strain into another cup, reheat if required, and sweeten with honey to taste.

ARMS

Many people lavish lots of attention on the care of their face and hands, but don't give the same care to the rest of their body. The arms, in particular, are often neglected.

Regular massage and exfoliation of the arms is essential. Massaging with a herbal lotion will improve the skin's elasticity and exfoliating will improve circulation and rid the skin of dead, clogging cells.

Make a simple and inexpensive but effective skin exfoliant at home by adding 2 tablespoons of medium ground oatmeal and 2 tablespoons of dried camomile to a muslin bath bag. If you don't have a bath bag, place the ingredients in the centre of a square of muslin, draw up the sides and tie with a piece of ribbon. As you rub your skin with this bag, you will actually feel the impurities and rough skin float away. The best time to exfoliate is while relaxing in an evening bath.

Don't forget your elbows. Scrub them daily with a soapy pumice stone (available from pharmacies) or a bath bag filled with the oatmeal mixture until all ingrained dirt has gone. Next, bleach the reddened skin by applying lemon juice and massage with a good natural moisturising cream or lotion.

ATHLETE'S FOOT

Apply cider vinegar over the affected area or apply a fungicide made by dissolving 1 part tea tree oil in 10 parts water.

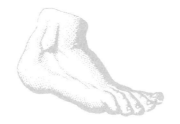

BACTERIA BUSTERS

The majority of essential oils are antiseptics and bactericides — in other words, they kill or inhibit the growth of bacteria. And, whichever way you use them, not only will they make your environment smell delightful, they'll make it safe as well. Essential oils can be used throughout the house, but they're a particular asset in the kitchen, bathroom and laundry.

KITCHEN AIR-FRESHENER SPRAY

Many smells are produced in the kitchen, an area that's often poorly ventilated so that not enough air circulates to clear away unpleasant aromas.

A fragrant air-freshener spray can be made to combat these smells. Use rosemary, lemon, eucalyptus, lavender or lime essential oils, singularly or in combination, to suit your taste. Dissolve 4 ml of the chosen oil or oils in 10 ml of methylated spirits, then add this mixture to 500 ml of distilled water in a pump-spray bottle. Shake well to mix and use as required on a fine mist setting.

OTHER KITCHEN-SMELL KILLERS

When washing out the fridge, freezer or oven, add 1 drop of lemon or bergamot oil to the final rinse water. This will deodorise without permeating the surface with an aroma.

For wiping down bench tops, cupboards, sinks, tiles or paintwork, add 1 drop of eucalyptus, lavender, lemon or thyme oil directly to the cloth or 7 drops in the rinse water.

BATHROOM

The important thing in bathrooms is to clear bacteria and viruses, especially if the toilet is located there. Use any of these essential oils — cinnamon, clove, lemon, eucalyptus, lavender, pine, niaouli, thyme or pine — in the final rinsing water when you wash all surfaces in the bathroom, including the bath, sink and toilet. These oils will kill germs and give the room a nice fragrance.

Television advertisements literally bombard our living rooms with an array of wonder products guaranteed to leave the bathroom and loo smelling like a pine grove or a breath of spring air. Yet the same results can be achieved with inexpensive, environmentally safe and easily found ingredients.

BATHROOM AIR-FRESHENER SPRAY

The following air-freshener spray will not only keep your bathroom and toilet fragrant and fresh, its disinfectant qualities will clear bacteria and viruses.

> *20 drops lavender oil*
> *5 drops lemon oil*
> *5 drops rosemary oil*
> *10 ml methylated spirits*

Dissolve the oils in the methylated spirits and add to a pump-spray bottle containing 500 ml of water. Use on a fine mist setting.

A strong antibacterial spray can be made with the following blend of oils:

> *5 drops bergamot oil*
> *10 drops lemon oil*
> *5 drops cinnamon oil*
> *10 drops citronella oil*
> *5 drops oregano oil*
> *10 drops sage oil*
> *20 drops eucalyptus oil*
> *10 drops thyme oil*
> *10 drops lavender oil*
> *10 ml methylated spirits*

Prepare as described above.

As an additional fragrance boost, a few drops of a concentrated fragrant oil or one of the previous concentrated blends can be placed on the cardboard tube inside the toilet paper roll before placing it in the holder.

LAUNDRY

To add a delicious fragrance to your wash, try putting 3 to 5 drops of lemongrass or lavender on a face cloth and drop it into the washing machine with your laundry. For a more exotic perfume

try ylang-ylang or neroli. In cold and flu season, add eucalyptus, rosemary or pine oil to the wash.

To perfume your clothes while ironing, add 3 to 6 drops of any of these oils to a pump-spray bottle containing 500 ml of distilled water and spray before ironing. You can also put the oils in the water compartment of your steam iron.

BAD BREATH

Add 2 drops of peppermint oil to a cup of warm water and gargle for a few minutes, then rinse. Repeat as often as needed. Or try chewing a fragrant cardamom pod two or three times a day.

If bad breath persists, it's wise to consult your health practitioner.

BATHROOM

See Bacteria Busters.

BATHS

See Dry Bathing and Herbal Baths.

BATH SALTS

Fragrant bath salts can be expensive to buy, yet can be easily and cheaply made at home. When you feel like pampering yourself, just add a couple of handfuls of these bath salts to your bath.

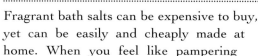

> *560 g bicarbonate of soda*
> *15 g dried lavender*
> *7 ml rosemary oil*
> *7 ml eucalyptus oil*

Thoroughly mix all ingredients together and store in an airtight jar.

To use, place 2 handfuls of the mixture in the centre of a muslin square, draw up the sides and tie with a piece of ribbon. Swirl around in the bath water until the contents are completely dissolved. When finished soaking, rub the muslin bag gently over your body until the scent of the lavender is exhausted.

BEE STING

Try to remove the sting by applying a cold camomile or honey compress to the area. Then put 1 drop of essential oil on a compress wrung out in cold water, cover the affected skin and leave in place for several hours if possible. Renew the oil three times a day for two days.

Ice applied to the affected area will also give relief.

See also Stings and Bites.

BITES

See Stings and Bites.

BLACK EYE

Soothe with a paste of bicarbonate soda and a cold cloth.

BLACKWOOD 'SOAP'

Use the leaves of the blackwood wattle (*Acacia melanoxylon*) to clean the dirtiest and greasiest hands.

Add two handfuls of leaves to either warm or cold water and rub vigorously between your hands.

BLANKET STAINS

Soak the blanket in cold salty water overnight then mix cornmeal with the water and rub vigorously into the stain. Allow to dry, then brush away and wash as normal.

This is especially effective for removing fresh blood stains.

BODY INSECT REPELLENTS

See Creepy Crawlies, Fly Repellents, Garden Sense and the individual insect pest entry.

BOILS

To encourage boils to come to a head, apply undiluted lemon juice or secure half a warm baked onion (with the centre layer removed to create a small dome) over the boil.

BOOKMARKS

Scraps of coloured or decorated paper, such as leftover Christmas wrap, can be turned into fragrant bookmarks in an enjoyable project for children on a wet weekend.

Cut to the length required, place a drop of a favourite essential oil on each one, and seal in individual polythene bags. Leave overnight for the aroma to infuse.

A papier-mâché bead can be strung with ribbon from the top of the bookmark so that it hangs out from the pages of the book.

BORAGE

Borage is one of the oldest known herbs used by the human race. Both the flowers and leaves have a therapeutic action.

Fresh, young leaves are an ideal addition to salads and also an excellent tonic for farm animals and poultry.

In the seventeenth century, a decoction of borage leaves, bran and barley was recommended as an additive to bath water to cleanse and soften the skin.

As a tea, borage exerts its benefits upon the liver, uterus, chest, stomach and bowels.

Leaves applied as a compress to the veins of the legs will relieve congestion and prevent varicose veins.

The flowers are very tasty and rich in both nectar and silicic acid, which aids in the healthy growth of hair, nails and the lining of mucous membranes.

BORAGE OINTMENT

Use this ointment for itchy and bleeding haemorrhoids.

2 tablespoons dried borage leaves
or 1 handful fresh leaves
100 ml glycerine

Put the ingredients in a small ceramic bowl and place this bowl in a pan of boiling water. Simmer over a low heat for 30 minutes. Remove, strain, and discard the herbs. Store in an airtight glass bottle and use as needed.

BUBBLE BATH

Bubble baths can be enjoyed by all members of the family, but are an especially great way for the kids to enjoy their bath while they wash the dirt and grime away. Rather than buying commercially made products, make your own at home.

2 teaspoons fragrant dried herb of choice
300 ml soft water, boiling
10 g pure white soap, grated
50 ml glycerine

Put the dried herb in a ceramic bowl and add the boiling water. Cover, infuse for three hours, strain through muslin, squeezing (and keeping) all liquid from the herbs.

Add the grated soap and herb water to an enamel or stainless steel pan and stir continuously over a medium heat until the soap has completely dissolved. Stir in the glycerine until well blended, remove from heat, cool, and store in a tightly capped bottle until the urge for a bubble bath occurs.

Pour a small amount into the bath while the water is running from the taps, and swish around to create the bubbles.

BURNS

See Honeysuckle and Tea Tree Oil.

BURNT-ON FOOD

To remove burnt-on food from aluminium saucepans, sprinkle with bicarbonate of soda and a dash of vinegar and bring to the boil. Wash when cool.

For enamel saucepans, sprinkle 2 tablespoons of bicarbonate of soda over the burnt-on food, then cover with boiling water and soak the pan overnight.

CAMOMILE OIL

See Conjunctivitis.

CAMOMILE TEA

Almost everyone is familiar with the herb camomile and its yellow and white daisy-like flowers that are used to make the popular tea. But are you aware that it is one of the safest and gentlest of all the herbs?

The Ancient Egyptians dedicated camomile to the sun, and the tea has been known and respected for centuries as being soothing and calming — German camomile (*Matricaria recutita*) being the most effective. In Europe many people drink a cup of this herbal tea as their customary nightcap to relax them before going to bed.

Camomile tea can be taken whenever needed, and used for any of the following ailments or reasons.

* *To calm the nerves.* Ideal for anyone at study time or when under stress, students and tired business people will benefit from a cup of camomile tea at the end of a day.
* *To help calm and settle a restless infant.* Add a few drops only to a baby's milk bottle; use occasionally.
* *To soothe cramp or colic in babies.* To make Infant's Gripe Water, put 1 teaspoon of dried camomile in an enamel or stainless steel pan, add 300 ml of boiling water and simmer for five minutes. Remove from heat, allow to cool, strain, add honey and use tepid in baby's bottle.
* *To relieve menstrual pain, nervous tension and to help prevent migraine headaches.*
* *To help in the treatment of red, inflamed eyes.* Add the cold tea to an eye-glass and bathe.
* *To help relax and soothe tired muscles.* Pour a strong brew of the tea into an evening bath.

Buy camomile tea bags from health-food stores and supermarkets.

CAR CARE

The once-humble automobile is a vital part of our lives nowadays yet, without doubt, it contributes greatly to the pollution levels, especially in our major cities.

This icon-like member of our modern society is lavished with a multitude of chemical products that clean, polish and deodorise, all of which are expensive and quite often unnecessary. Why not try the following environmentally safe and inexpensive alternatives to the array of commercially available car-care products?

WASHING

Use a bucket and water only — do not leave water running from the hose — and avoid the use of phosphate detergents. Dissolve soft soap (available from pharmacies) in a bucket of water as an effective and suitable alternative to detergents containing phosphate. Wipe over with a chamois cloth to remove any film.

POLISHING

Give the car a normal wash, let it dry, then sprinkle cornflour over the duco. Rub it in, then polish it off for a brilliant sheen.

GREASE STAINS ON UPHOLSTERY

Remove grease stains on upholstery can by rubbing bicarbonate soda into the spot, then brushing it away.

ODOUR ELIMINATION

Unpleasant odours, including the smell of stale cigarettes, can be eliminated by placing a container of dry bicarbonate soda in the car. To remove odours from vinyl seats and lining panels, wash with a solution of bicarbonate soda and warm water.

Quite often the interior of new cars will smell strongly of plastic. If you find this offensive, wash the vinyl and plastic surfaces with

a solution of 1 tablespoon of vinegar to 1 cup of water, rinse well, then leave the car in the sun with the doors open while it dries.

GLASS AND CHROME CLEANERS

All glass and chrome surfaces can be cleaned using a solution of 10 ml vinegar to 500 ml of hot water. Buff off with wads of newspaper. Chrome will also come clean to a gleaming surface with bicarbonate soda. Simply sprinkle it onto a damp cloth and rub the surface clean.

REMOVING REGISTRATION STICKERS

Old registration stickers and other transfers can be removed without creating a mess of small scrapings by using a wet piece of plastic cling-film. Place the film over the transfer, leave for 30 minutes and peel off.

BATTERY CARE

Remove the encrustation that forms on car battery terminals by mixing 2 teaspoons of bicarbonate soda with a litre of water and generously brushing each terminal with it. Since the solution is slightly alkaline, it will neutralise the acid.

RADIATOR CLEANER

Drain the cooling system and flush it out with running water. Close drain outlets, add 200 grams washing soda to the radiator, fill with clean water, and run the car for short distances only for three days. Then drain the washing soda water from the system, flush thoroughly, and fill with clean water.

Note. Do not use this method if your car has an aluminium head or the cooling system is in poor condition.

CARPET DEODORISER

In days of yesteryear, aromatic grasses and highly fragrant herbs and flowers were placed under rugs and mats so that when they were walked upon, their aroma was released. Today, most homes have wall-to-wall carpeting and this type of practice would be impractical. However, carpets and living rooms, or any room for that matter, can be kept fragrantly fresh with a easy-to-make carpet-freshener powder. It is made simply by blending essential oils with a natural powder such as bicarbonate of soda or kaolin (china clay – available from pharmacies or potters' suppliers), and used in exactly the same way as commercial products.

To make your deodorant powder, simply add 1 drop of a chosen essential oil to every tablespoon of base powder, and mix thoroughly in a blender. How much you make up depends on your requirements. Once made, store your powder in an airtight jar or sealable plastic bag in a dry, cool, dark spot for 24 hours before use (allowing it to fully absorb the aromatic oil), then sprinkle it on your carpet, leave for a few minutes and vacuum it up.

Lavender is my oil of choice because my family likes the scent. It has antibacterial properties, makes an excellent deodorant and repels insects such as moths and silverfish.

The made-up powder can be stored indefinitely in an airtight glass jar.

CARPET STAINS

See Eucalyptus Oil.

CATARRH

My grandmother would swear by her leek and ginger soup for the relief of catarrh associated with cold and flu.

Leek and Ginger Soup
Trim, rinse and slice three leeks and grate sufficient fresh ginger to make 1 tablespoon. Gently heat 1 tablespoon of olive oil in a large pan and saute the leeks for about ten minutes without browning. Add the grated ginger and 1 litre of water. Cover, bring to the boil, and allow to simmer for 20 minutes until the leeks are tender. Season to taste with fresh parsley and thyme.

CHAPPED LIPS

Apply the following lip balm whenever required to keep your lips moist and supple, and to prevent them from chapping or splitting.

Melt 15 grams of beeswax in a double pan over a medium heat. When completely liquified, stir in 50 ml almond oil, 10 ml

wheatgerm oil, 5 ml jojoba oil and 40 ml of distilled water until well blended. Remove from heat and pour into a ceramic bowl. Add 6 drops of friar's balsam and 5 drops each of camomile and rose oils. Beat until cool and creamy. Store in a sterilised glass jar.

See also Skin (Protection).

CHICKENS

Having chickens in the backyard isn't everyone's idea of bliss, and some local councils won't allow it, anyway. But if you have a large enough yard, and it's okay with the council, and your neighbours don't mind, think about running three or four chooks.

The most efficient chicken run for the suburbs is the moveable ark or A-frame, with one end covered for perches and laying boxes and the rest covered with wire netting. My father used this system for many years to weed and fertilise his vegetable garden. The run has no base and is lifted and moved around as desired.

Laying boxes are built against the covered end wall with outside hatches for access. Once the chickens have handed over their bounty, you can let them out to scratch around for a while — they love to look for worms in the compost, and will be turning it over at the same time. However, make sure they don't have access to your young seedlings or the vegetable patch.

Free-range chickens will only need organic wheat and a small amount of mash each day, as well as plenty of fresh water and shade in summer. Keep their living quarters clean, grow a few pots of southernwood (*Artemisia abrotanum*) nearby and you won't be bothered with lice and other pests. Buy only healthy stock from a reputable dealer, and only chickens that haven't been debeaked.

Pullets are usually sold when three months old at point of lay. Check the Yellow Pages for the nearest free-range chicken farm; the birds will be healthier than the mass produced variety.

Which to get? Leghorns seem to be the most popular choice and are good layers, but you may prefer the coloured varieties, such as Rhode Island Red and Australorp.

FOWL MANURE

Four to six chickens will produce between 60 to 90 kg of manure per year. In addition, the scratching litter from the pen is excellent for top dressing or incorporating into the garden soil.

Poultry manure can also be used to make liquid manure, or it can be added to the compost heap.

CHILBLAINS

Mix together 1 tablespoon each of honey and glycerin, 1 teaspoon of rose water, the white of an egg, and sufficient flour to make a paste. Wash the affected area with warm water; dry and spread on the paste. Cover with a piece of sterile linen or cotton bandage.

Soaking your feet in potato-peel water is also reputed to be a remedy for chilblains.

CHOPPING BOARD

To clean a kitchen chopping board, simply sprinkle salt onto the surface and scour with a damp cloth. Salt has excellent disinfecting qualities.

CHRISTMAS

See Xmas.

CLEANERS

Most cleaning chores used to be carried out using whatever ingredients were close at hand. Those simple solutions from yesteryear are just as effective and safe today. So next time you're shopping, forget about the bewildering array of products made for almost every household purpose and get back to the basics.

ALL-PURPOSE LIQUID CLEANSERS

Effective, all-purpose, environmentally friendly houselhold liquid cleaners can be made quickly and inexpensively from easily obtained ingredients.

Mix thoroughly together 4 litres of hot water, 100 ml of household ammonia*, 100 ml of white vinegar and 200 grams of bicarbonate soda. Store in a tightly sealed bottle.

Not only will this all-purpose cleaner be suitable for most cleaning chores around the home, it will strip floor wax, dissolve dirt, grease and resinous substances, and clean silver, glass, sinks, bathroom surfaces and drainpipes, stoves, microwave ovens, refrigerators and other whitegoods.

If you prefer a fragrant liquid cleanser with the added benefits of essential oils, dissolve 25 drops each of lavender, thyme, juniper and eucalyptus oils in 20 ml of methylated spirits. Blend this mixture and 2 tablespoons of borax with 1 litre of warm water. Store in a sealed bottle for future use. Apply with a clean, soft cloth.

*Household ammonia contains about 3.7% ammonia and when diluted further, as in the this cleaner, is not environmentally dangerous. Once dispersed, it converts quickly to neutral salts.

BATHROOM CLEANER

To make a disinfectant cleaner for use on tiles, baths, basins and toilets, use the back of a large metal spoon to thoroughly blend together 25 drops each of lavender, pine, juniper and eucalyptus oils and 10 drops of thyme oil with 2 cups of bicarbonate soda. Store in a suitable container and use as required, applying with a damp cloth and wiping off with a clean, soft cloth.

BICARBONATE SODA

Bicarbonate soda on a wet sponge is an economical cleaner for windows and stainless steel, chrome and laminate surfaces. Polish off with a soft cloth.

Made into a moist paste, it will remove tarnish from silver. Apply with a damp sponge, rub until clean, rinse, and buff to a gloss.

Mixed with warm water, bicarbonate soda makes a gentle but effective cleanser for refrigerator and freezer surfaces.

KITCHEN CLEANER

Using the back of a large metal spoon, thoroughly blend 15 drops each of rosemary and thyme oils with 1 cup of bicarbonate soda. Apply with a damp cloth to clean kitchen tiles, bench tops and all other kitchen surfaces. Wipe off with a clean, soft cloth.

LAVENDER CLEANSER

This aromatic paste is ideal for cleaning and disinfecting bathroom sinks, tubs, shower recesses and tiles, and anywhere there is built-up grime or mould.

Place 1 tablespoon each of dried (or fresh) lavender buds and rosemary leaves in an enamel or stainless steel pan, add 300 ml of water, bring to the boil and reduce to a simmer for 30 minutes (adjusting water if necessary). Strain through muslin cloth, squeezing and keeping all liquid from the herbs. Blend 2 parts of this herbal liquid to 1 part of white vinegar. (Reserve a small amount of the herbal mixture.) Add 1 cup of pure soap flakes or 1 cup of grated pure laundry soap to a pan with just enough of the herbal and vinegar liquid to cover. Melt the soap flakes over a medium heat, stirring constantly, then add 75 grams of precipitated chalk (calcium carbonate) and more of the herbal liquid to form a soft, thick paste. Store in a wide-mouthed container with a lid. Apply with a cloth, then rinse off.

TIMBER FURNITURE CLEANER AND POLISH

This liquid polish will clean and polish all timber surfaces. People with asthma and those who suffer from dust allergies will appreciate the way it picks up the dust, preventing it from being flicked into the air.

Thoroughly blend together 125 ml (½ cup) strained lemon juice, 250 ml (1 cup) raw linseed oil and 10 drops essential oil of lemon. Apply with a slightly moistened soft rag.

See also Jasmine Furniture Polish, Lemon Timber Polish, Polishing Cloth and Polish.

VINEGAR

Three-quarters of a litre of white vinegar added to a medium size bucket of warm water makes a universal cleaner for almost

everything: glass, mirrors, ceramic tiles, enamel surfaces, chrome, refrigerators, washing machines and even floors. To clean window sills and remove mould, soak a cloth in this vinegar and water solution and wipe over.

Simmer a strong solution of white vinegar in aluminium pots for 20 minutes to remove stubborn stains from them. Wash and use a wooden spoon to scrape. To clean burnt saucepans, sprinkle with bicarbonate soda and a dash of vinegar and bring to the boil. Wash when cool.

Stainless steel can be cleaned with a cloth dampened with vinegar — rinse thoroughly.

To clean the inside of plastic electric jugs or kettles, add 1 cup of white vinegar, top up with water, boil for 10 minutes, and rinse out well.

See also Bacteria Busters, Horsetail, Lemon Juice, and Salt.

CLOTHES

When winter is over, precious woollens, other warm clothes and blankets are usually put into storage — and forgotten about until the following year. In the meantime, without adequate protection, they can become a banquet for moth larvae.

Commercially made sprays and moth balls are available to protect your clothes and other woollen items — but both options are poisonous and should be avoided. There are safe, natural alternatives that will work just as well.

Herbs have been used for centuries as protection against clothing moths. Add the herbs to small muslin bags and place them in drawers and cupboards among woollens and other clothes. They can also be placed in the pockets of suits and jackets or hung on coat hangers or wardrobe rails.

MOTH-REPELLENT BAGS

A suitable repellent can be made by mixing together, in a large ceramic bowl, 25 grams each of dried rosemary, wormwood and lavender, 15 grams of freshly crushed cloves and 2 tablespoons of orrisroot powder. Mix with your hands to ensure good combination. Add the herbal mix to a plastic bag, seal to make airtight and leave to cure in a dry, dark place for four to six weeks.

Give the mix a good shake every second day. When ready, place a spoonful in the centre of a muslin square and tie with a ribbon or, if you're more resourceful, sew muslin pouches.

Check the scent of your moth bags every six months — make up a new batch if they're no longer potent.

OTHER MOTH REPELLERS

Small cotton-wool balls dipped in essential oils (try lavender, lemongrass, camphor or rosemary) and put between clothes in drawers will repel moths. So will drawer liners cut from blotting or other absorbent paper, dotted with your chosen oil and then brushed over with orrisroot powder to fix the scent.

Dried orange or lemon peel scattered in drawers and cupboards will also act as a deterrent. So will a cloth soaked in natural turpentine rubbed thoroughly over all internal wood surfaces of drawers and wardrobes, including joints and crevices.

MOTH-REPELLENT RINSE

Blankets can also be protected with a moth repellent infusion added to the final washing machine rinse. If washing by hand, rinse the blankets well in clean water and then do a final rinse using the herbal infusion described below.

Put 4 teaspoons of dried lavender and 2 teaspoons each of dried rosemary and wormwood in a ceramic bowl and add 600 ml of boiling water. Cover, steep overnight, strain through muslin cloth, and add the liquid to your final rinse.

See also Bacteria Busters, Eucalyptus Oil, Laundry Sense, Lavender (Lavender Wool Wash) and Rust (Clothing).

COLDS

INHALATIONS

Add 2 drops each of pine, eucalyptus and cypress oil to the bath water, lie back and inhale deeply.

For a steam inhalation, add 1 drop each of the same oils to a bowl of hot water, close your eyes and breathe deeply.

Place 1 drop each of thyme, peppermint, eucalyptus and clove oils on a tissue or handkerchief, and inhale deeply from the tissue or handkerchief whenever possible.

When you have a cold, massage around the chest, neck and sinus area (forehead, nose and cheekbones) with the following oil blend: 1 drop of lemon oil, 2 drops of eucalyptus oil and 3 drops of rosemary oil with 1 teaspoon of almond oil.

See also Catarrh, Onion (Onion Syrup), and Tea Tree Oil.

HERBAL TEA

A herbal tea made by combining equal parts of peppermint, elderflower and yarrow will help to alleviate the symptoms of cold, fever and influenza. Steep 1 teaspoon of the dried herb mixture in a cup of boiling water for 10 minutes, strain, reheat, sweeten with honey and drink as hot as possible three to four times daily.

Peppermint is rich in volatile oils, including menthol, which help to relieve head and chest congestion. Taken on its own, peppermint tea is very beneficial in reducing fever; its effect is increased when combined with yarrow flowers. Peppermint also helps to allay nausea and acts as a soothing sedative to induce relaxation and sleep.

Elderflower is rich in the mineral salt potassium chloride — a vital salt for dealing with the second stage congestion of colds and flu. It has a relaxing, calming and blood purifying effect, and also helps to induce perspiration.

Yarrow is a tonic and stimulant, serving to reinforce the body's vitality and strength. It is useful in mild fevers, producing perspiration and opening the pores of the skin. (Free perspiration encourages the elimination of toxins and waste products from the body. Poor elimination is one of the primary factors leading to the development of colds, fevers and flu.) This herb also contains the mineral salt iron phosphate, which is especially effective in helping to treat infectious colds and fevers that are aggravated by bacteria.

To accentuate the action of this herbal tea and speed up its beneficial effects, add a pinch of cayenne pepper, which is both stimulating and warming, and acts as a catalyst.

SHIVERY COLDS

A clove of garlic taken three times a day with meals will help to alleviate cold symptoms, and is even more effective when taken in conjunction with half a teaspoon of horseradish powder in some warm water.

FEVERISH COLDS

Put the juice of half a lemon into a cup of boiling water, add a peppermint tea bag and steep for five minutes, then sweeten with honey. Reheat if required and drink three to six times a day.

REFRESHING A SICK ROOM

See Floral Vinegar.

SPECIAL BATH FOR COLDS

The properties of the essential oils used in this bath blend will exert their therapeutic value through the inhaled vapour, clearing the head and helping to relieve the miseries of a cold. Close all windows and the bathroom door for maximum effect.

Run the bath water as hot as you can stand it and, when it's almost full, add 2 drops each of thyme and tea tree oils, 1 drop of eucalyptus oil and 3 drops of lemon oil. Swish the water around to ensure they are thoroughly blended.

Sit with your knees up and your head between them so that you can fully inhale the restorative vapours. As the water cools, slosh it all over your body.

If you feel really ill, nauseated or running a fever, it is advisable not to take a full bath; instead, add the blend to a bowl of water and use to sponge the skin under your arms and around your genital area. Inhale the steam from the bowl until there is no more aromatic vapour.

PROTECTING CHILDREN FROM WINTER COLDS

We all know how miserable and unpleasant it is to have a cold, but it must be twice as bad for toddlers and young children who quite often don't understand what's happening.

The front-line attack is to build up a child's body's resistance to infection. A wholefood diet that includes plenty of fresh fruit and vegetables and fresh herbs, including garlic, will help the body systems combat harmful bacteria and viruses.

Garlic is especially useful in building up the body's resistance, as it contains vitamins A, B and C, and copper, sulphur, manganese, iron and calcium. It is also considered to be a natural antibiotic if taken in large enough amounts.

Rosehip tea, reputed to be high in vitamin C, can also be used to build resistance to colds and other infections.

WHEN THE COLD STRIKES A CHILD

Most colds will also respond to other fruity treats. Add the juice of half a lemon to a cup of boiling water and sweeten with honey. Administer three times daily.

Essential oils can also be used and are very efficient at destroying harmful bacteria and viruses. They are especially useful when toddlers and babies have colds. You can simply place a small bowl of boiling water to which you have added the following blend, under the child's bed or cot, but not directly under the baby's head. The steam will rise, releasing the aroma into the room.

Mix together 50 drops each of eucalyptus, tea tree and lavender oils and store in an airtight, amber-coloured glass bottle. Add 3 drops of the blend to the bowl of hot water at night, and again during the day. If the child is having a lot of difficulty in breathing bvecause of nasal stuffiness, place 2 drops of the oil blend on a cotton-wool ball and place it under the edge of his or her pillow.

One drop of the oil blend can also be added to a baby's bath water. For one- to five-year-olds, add 2 drops to the bath.

Vaporising is also effective for relieving a stuffy or blocked-up nose in older children. Moisten a small sponge with boiling water and add a few drops of the essential oil blend. Place the sponge in a dish in their room, and moisten it with boiling water twice a day, refreshing it with a few drops of the oil twice a week.

It must be remembered, however, that colds can be the forerunner of something more serious. So if the child has a high temperature, is feverish, off food, crying a lot and won't settle, have him or her checked by your medical practitioner.

NATURAL MEDICINE

The following natural medicine can be given to children by the tablespoonful twice a day to help build resistance or to alleviate the miseries of a cold.

Slice 500 grams of peeled onions into small rings. Put these in an enamel or stainless steel saucepan and add 2 litres of water, 80 grams of honey, and 500 grams of brown sugar. Simmer slowly for four hours, cool, and strain through a fine sieve. Bottle the liquid for future use.

COLD SORES

A good diet will help to prevent cold sores. Include plenty of fresh fruit and vegetables, beans (pulses), chicken, fish and brewer's yeast. Avoid eating bread, biscuits, oats, red meat, chocolate, sugar, coffee and hot spices.

See also Tea Tree Oil.

COLOGNE

Fragrant flowers and herbs can be made into sweet-smelling colognes that will lift your spirits, make you feel special, and cool and refresh your skin during hot summer days and nights. Splash them on your body after a shower or bath, or anytime you need to feel refreshed.

LEMON COLOGNE

This cologne will not only refresh you, but impart a beautiful lemon scent, too.

2 cups (tightly-packed) fresh lemon balm leaves
1 litre vodka
500 ml distilled water
70 drops essential oil of lime
150 drops essential oil of lemon

Steep the lemon balm in the vodka for fourteen days. Mix the lemon alcohol mixture with the distilled water and essential oils and allow to stand for a further ten days. Drip through filter paper and store in a tightly-sealed glass bottle.

ORIENTAL COLOGNE

This exotic cologne will leave your skin feeling fragrant and refreshed, and is made by simply infusing a combination of scented herbs and spices.

6 tablespoons chopped angelica leaves and stalks
6 tablespoons chopped lemon balm leaves
15 g coriander seeds, crushed
1 nutmeg, grated
2 tablespoons cloves
4 x 25 mm sticks of cinnamon
300 ml vodka

Put the herbs and spices in a large, wide-mouthed, glass jar, and add the vodka. Seal and shake vigorously. Leave in a warm place for three weeks, shaking every day. Strain through fine muslin and then drip through filter paper into a suitable glass bottle; bottles with ground glass stoppers are ideal and look attractive on bathroom vanities or bedroom dressing tables.

Splash on your body after a bath or shower.

COMBS

Combs can be cleaned quickly and effectively by placing them in hot water and sprinkling over a teaspoon of bicarbonate of soda. Leave for a few minutes and then rinse.

COMFREY FERTILISER

See Garden Fertilisers.

COMPOST TEA

We all know that composting is good for the garden, but did you know that compost can be applied as a liquid tea? If you give it some thought, it makes sense to give your garden a liquid boost, particularly during dry weather when plants are starved both for food and water. Since most nutrients in compost dissolve quickly and readily in water, they can be quickly distributed to needy plant roots.

To make compost tea, add about a 10 cm layer of mature compost to a bucket of water. Allow to stand for 48 hours, stirring occasionally, then strain through coarsely woven cloth.

Apply the undiluted 'tea' to the soil over the plant roots, or spray or sprinkle over the leaves of plants. Repeat every two weeks for flowers and vegetables, and monthly for shrubs. Compost tea is especially good for leafy vegetables such as silver beet, spinach, cabbage and lettuce.

Use it on bare spots on your lawn, on trees that have just been transplanted and on indoor plants that need perking up. Mix a handful of wood ash to the solution before using and it can double as a natural insecticide.

See also Garden Fertilisers and Green Manuring.

COOLING

See Summer Cooling.

CONJUNCTIVITIS

To help in the treatment of conjunctivitis, add 1 drop of camomile oil to 1 teaspoon of witch hazel (buy it from pharmacies) and mix thoroughly. Add this solution to 30 ml of rosewater and stand for eight hours, then strain through coffee-filter paper. Use with a compress on the eyelids (be sure to keep your eyes closed).

CORNS

Rub the corn with a crushed garlic clove every night, or put a sliver of garlic on the corn and hold it on your foot with sticking plaster. Another remedy is to apply freshly crushed marigold (*Calendula officinalis*) leaves to the corn morning and night.

COUCH GRASS FERTILISER

See Garden Fertilisers.

COUGHS

Mix the juice from half a lemon with 2 tablespoons of honey and administer every 15 minutes.

CREEPY-CRAWLIES

Natural alternatives are an altogether better way of dealing with the creepy-crawlies that invade our living spaces. One of the easiest ways of dealing with these unwanted visitors, and deterring them from biting, is by using the appropriate essential herbal oils.

Essential oils are not only useful worn on the body as repellents, but can also be used to spray inside the house without fear of polluting the air we breathe or endangering the health of our family or friends.

Insects have a very short life and come and go in waves at particular times of the year. During the spring and summer months, flies, mosquitoes, midges and sandflies can become extremely bothersome, especially when you are enjoying outdoor activities on warm summer evenings. However something as simple as applying lavender oil to exposed skin will keep these biting and annoying pests at bay.

PERSONAL BODY REPELLENT

Dissolve 10 drops of lavender oil in 5 ml (1 teaspoon) of vodka and blend this mixture with three-quarters of a cup of water. Store in a tightly sealed bottle or a small plastic perfume atomiser. Simply dab or spray onto exposed skin and rub well in.

If you're one of those individuals who seems to overly attract biting creepy-crawlies, you can adjust your repellent by increasing the amount of essential oil in the mix — an extra 10 to 15 drops should be sufficient.

EXTRA-STRONG REPELLENT

Make an extra-strong body repellent, that can also be sprayed inside the home, by dissolving 3 ml of oil of cloves and 5 ml (1 teaspoon) each of lavender and eucalyptus oil in 150 ml of perfumer's alcohol or vodka. Blend with 200 ml of distilled water and apply to exposed skin when necessary.

When using as a household repellent spray, add the mixture to a pump-spray bottle and use on a fine mist setting.

HOUSEHOLD REPELLENT SPRAY

Another effective repellent spray, and the one most often used in my household, consists of 1.5 ml each of lavender and citronella oils dissolved in 10 ml (2 teaspoons) of methylated spirits and mixed with 500 ml of water. Use in a pump-spray bottle on a fine mist setting.

OTHER TRICKS TO KEEP THE PESTS AT BAY

To deter night-time pests, install red lights in outdoor entertainment areas where you eat and cook — a white light installed some way off will help to attract pests away from you. Avoid using outdoor electric insect 'zappers', as they also kill large numbers of 'beneficial' insects — the ones that don't bite and annoy, and keep other pests under control.

Burning insect repellent candles, such as lavender, eucalyptus and citronella, will also help to keep the nasties from spoiling your outdoor evening activities. Repellent candles are also effective for indoor use.

See also Fly Repellents, Garden Sense, Insect Pests and the individual insect entries.

CUCUMBER COLD CREAM

This is an ideal natural skin-care lotion for oily skin. It's also great for soothing skin after a day outdoors in the sun or wind.

> *60 ml fresh cucumber juice*
> *60 ml witch-hazel solution (from pharmacies)*
> *1 teaspoon camphor water (available from your pharmacy)*

Peel the cucumber, process the flesh in a blender and strain the juice through clean muslin. Combine 60 ml of the juice with the other ingredients and store in an airtight bottle in the refrigerator. Shake well before use.

See also Herbal Skin Care and Skin.

CUTLERY

Remove stains from steel cutlery by rubbing with the cut side of a raw potato, then washing in warm soapy water and polishing.

Most food stains can also be removed with a paste of bicarbonate soda. Rub firmly, rinse off and dry with a soft cloth.

See also Cleaners (Vinegar).

CUTS AND ABRASIONS

Add 2 to 3 drops of tea tree or lavender oil to a bowl of warm water for an excellent antiseptic. Wash the wound thoroughly and apply the tea tree or lavender solution with a clean cotton wool ball three times a day.

Apple cider vinegar (undiluted) is also an excellent antiseptic.

See also Tea Tree Oil.

CYSTITIS

Drink a glass of raw beetroot juice morning and night if troubled by a urinary tract infection. Bicarbonate of soda is also a helpful first aid remedy for a sudden attack of cystitis. Add a level teaspoon of bicarbonate soda to a glass of water, and drink once an hour for three hours to relieve acute symptoms.

Another helpful remedy is old-fashioned barley water. Barley is well known for its anti-inflammatory action on the genitourinary tract. To make your own barley water, simmer 50 grams of unrefined barley (from health-food stores) in 1 litre of water for 40 minutes. Cool, strain and drink over 24 hours.

If the problem persists, consult your health practitioner.

DANDRUFF

The telltale flakes of dead skin cells scattered on your shoulders are a good indication that the skin on your head, and your hair, are in bad condition. It's time to take action if you brush your hair thoroughly in the morning and brush your shoulders before leaving the house but, by the middle of the day, the embarrassing white flakes are back.

Food allergies and sugary diets can often promote dandruff, so cut down on excessively spicy foods, too much fat and sugar, very starchy white flour products and alcohol (spirits in particular). Eat plenty of raw vegetables and fruits, vegetable oils and nuts, lean meat and fish.

Essential oils will help relieve and even banish dandruff once and for all. Massage rosemary or nutmeg oils into the scalp and use the after-shampoo conditioning rinse described below.

CONDITIONING RINSE

Every night before going to bed, massage a teaspoon of the following mixture into your scalp only.

Blend together 15 drops each of jojoba oil and evening primrose oil, 5 drops of carrot oil and 3 drops of cypress oil. Store in an amber-coloured glass bottle for no longer than two months.

See also Herbal Hair Care.

DANDYADE

This refreshing fizzy, summer drink is made from dandelion petals.

1 cup of fresh dandelion petals
juice and rind of 1 lemon
half a cup of brown sugar
500 ml boiling water

Cut green parts from dandelion flowers. Place the green parts in an enamel pot with lemon juice, lemon rind and brown sugar. Add boiling water and leave to infuse until cold. Strain through fine muslin, squeezing all liquid from the flowers, and refrigerate. Dilute with mineral water as required.

DIET

HERBS IN THE DIET

Throughout history, the use of herbs in food has contributed a great deal towards human health. They are excellent companions in any salad and, as well as being a healthy treat, will give extra zest to summer meals. Dried and ground into a powder, they can be used as natural spices for vegetable dishes.

By including herbs and natural supplements in our diet, we not only aid our health, but also make eating rewarding.

During summer, most people enjoy barbecuing, and fresh herbs can be used in many ways to enhance the flavour of whatever you cook. Try some of the following ideas.

* Throw herbs on the coals when grilling on the barbecue and, if possible, cover the grill with a foil tent to allow the spicy smoke to penetrate the food. Use stalks of fresh savory (*Satureja hortensis*), sage, rosemary, whole star anise, fennel or dried basil seed pods.
* Skewer herbs between pieces of meat or fish when barbecuing kebabs. Bay leaf works well with fish, fresh dill with lamb, and basil with beef.
* Wrap fresh corn or potatoes in foil, slip in a sprig of marjoram, and roast on the barbecue.
* Grill fish wrapped in foil with a slice of lemon and a sprig of dill or a sliver or two of garlic.

A barbecue's not a barbecue without summer salad vegetables. Add fresh herbs to liven up the taste of your salads.

* Tear nasturtium, sorrel, cress, young dandelion leaves and basil leaves into pieces and mix with tossed greens. Mince strong herbs such as savoury, dill and thyme.
* Green fennel seeds tossed in salads and coleslaw will add pockets of spice.
* Fruit salad is even more cool and refreshing served on a bed of freshly picked mint.
* Garnish shredded lettuce with fresh oregano.

Crush the fresh herbs in the palm of your hand to release the flavour before adding them to the other vegetables.

LEMON BALM AND MUSHROOM SALAD

The ideal accompaniment to summer barbecues.
Chop 2 apples, 100 grams raw mushrooms, 4 celery stalks and half an onion, and thoroughly mix together. Place on a bed of lettuce, sprinkle over a little finely grated cheese and red capsicum. Garnish with 2 tablespoons of freshly chopped lemon balm leaves.

Add fresh young dandelion leaves, sorrel or purslane (*Portulaca sativa*) to make your salad a little more interesting and nourishing. Tear into small pieces and mix with the other ingredients.

See also Minerals, Nutrition and Vitamins.

DIGESTION

Many of the herbs best known and mostly used for flavouring and seasoning also stimulate the flow of digestive juices in the stomach and intestines. Classic herb and food partnerships in cooking reflect this: rosemary helps the digestion of fatty lamb; fennel assists the digestion of oily fish; horseradish aids in the digestion of beef.

Aromatic seeds such as aniseed, cardamom, caraway, dill and fennel are useful digestives. A tablespoon of ground aniseed boiled in a cup of milk and drunk twice a day will improve digestion. To increase the flow of saliva, add a teaspoon of cardamom to the aniseed drink and take half an hour before meals.

See also Dill Water, Indigestion and Onion (Onion Syrup).

DILL WATER

Dill water helps the body to absorb food and aids digestion. It is also excellent for calming hiccups, and will help induce restful sleep. It is free of harmful effects and can be given safely to young children.

25 g dill seed
1 tablespoon honey
300 ml hot water

Crush the dill seed with a mortar and pestle, or with the back of a metal spoon on a chopping board, then soak for three to four hours in the water. Strain and sweeten with the honey. Sip a small amount after meals twice daily.

DISHES

To wash dishes, use pure soap in an old-fashioned soap shaker; these are still available at many hardware and kitchen stores.

To eliminate fishy smells from your dishes, sprinkle a little powdered mustard into the washing water.

DISINFECTANT

Herbs and essential oils are useful as household disinfectants. As well as their wonderful aromatic qualities, they also have antibacterial, antifungal and antiviral properties. Any of the following herbs can be used, and are listed in descending order of their antiseptic power: lemon, tea tree, thyme, bergamot, juniper, clove, lavender, peppermint, rosemary, sandalwood and eucalyptus.

To make a disinfectant from essential oils, dissolve 20 to 30 drops of your selected essential oil in 5 ml (1 teaspoon) of methylated spirits and mix this with 1 litre of distilled water. Store in an airtight plastic or glass bottle.

Alternatively, place 4 tablespoons of a selected dried herb in an enamel or stainless steel pan, cover with 1½ cups of distilled water, bring to the boil and simmer for ten minutes. Remove from heat, cover and steep for two hours. Strain through muslin cloth, squeezing and keeping all liquid from the herbs. Add sufficient distilled water to the herb liquid to make 1 litre. Add 40 ml of methylated spirits, mix thoroughly and store in an airtight bottle.

See also Bacteria Busters.

DISINFECTANT FLOOR CLEANER

See Eucalyptus Oil.

DOG WASH

Regular use of this wash will keep your dog's coat clean and help to control fleas.

soft soap, sufficient (available from pharmacies)
30 g powdered derris (available from garden supply stores)
5 litres warm water

Mix sufficient soft soap with the warm water until you have a soapy solution that lathers well. Add the derris powder, stirring until it has completely dissolved.

Wash the animal thoroughly and rinse with clean, warm water.

See also Eucalyptus Oil.

DRINKS

SUMMER DRINKS WITH A HERBAL TWIST

Do you enjoy the taste of herbs as a garnish or zesty addition to food? Well, don't stop there. Add herbs to your favourite beverages for a refreshing change.

Try lemonade with lemon balm, tomato juice with oregano or basil, mineral water with rose geranium, white wine with borage blossoms floating on top, or refreshing iced herbal tea with tangy mint. And perk up the ice cubes you add to these drinks by freezing a sprig of mint or a borage flower in each cube.

Experiment with the many delicious ways to use fragrant herbs and flowers in drinks.

ELDERFLOWER 'CHAMPAGNE'

This is a favourite non-alcoholic herbal beverage in my family.

Dissolve 875 grams of sugar in 2 cups of hot distilled water. Pour into an enamel or stainless steel pan with 4 large fresh elderflower heads, 2 tablespoons of white wine vinegar, the juice and rind (remove the pith and cut into quarters) of 1 lemon, and 4 litres of water. Stir, cover and leave for four to five days. Strain off the liquid into clean screw-top bottles and leave for six days or until effervescing. Serve chilled.

MINT JULEP

This one's another of our family favourites that's easy to make and very refreshing on hot summer days.

Wash 5 handfuls of fresh mint, place in a ceramic or enamel basin and cover with 1 cup of sugar and the strained juice of 5 lemons. Allow to stand for two hours, stir and transfer to a large glass jug. Add six ice cubes, 1.5 litres of ginger ale and fresh sprigs of mint. Serve in tall glasses.

ICED HERBAL TEA

Drink it any time of the day. Iced herbal tea is particularly refreshing on a hot summer day mixed with chilled mineral water or fresh fruit juice. Add a long, leafy stalk of the appropriate herb for added flavour.

To make the tea, steep 1 tablespoon of fresh, or 1 to 2 teaspoons of dried, leafy herbs for each cup of hot water. Infuse for five minutes, then chill.

Try herbs such as camomile, mint, marjoram, lemon balm, lemon verbena, scented geraniums or lemongrass.

CINNAMON TEA

Try this delicious, spicy tea morning or night as a refreshing alternative to conventional tea. Put 250 grams of white clover blossoms and 1 large cinnamon stick, broken into pieces, in an enamel or stainless steel pan and add 500 ml of boiling water. Bring to a simmer, add 1 teaspoon of finely grated orange rind and cook gently for five minutes. Remove from heat, cover, and infuse for a further five minutes. Strain and sweeten to taste with honey.

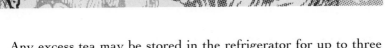

Any excess tea may be stored in the refrigerator for up to three days and warmed before drinking.

THERAPEUTIC TEAS

Lemongrass
An excellent first herbal tea to try, if you haven't already enjoyed the experience. Lemongrass is very palatable and refreshing, rich in vitamin A and is considered ideal for purifying the skin and refining its texture.

Peppermint
With its refreshing and delicately fruity taste, peppermint is by far one of the best known of the herbal teas. It acts as a tonic and is reputed to relieve chest congestion and congestion in any other part of the body. It relieves indigestion, flatulence and digestive disturbances, and acts as a mild sedative when taken prior to going to bed. Add a slice of lemon and some honey and drink it to help ease a nagging headache. Blended with equal parts of yarrow and elderflower, it is a time-tested remedy for colds.

Lemon Balm
Drinking lemon balm tea during the hot weather will help lessen the effects of exhaustion. It's very refreshing and makes an excellent cold drink when mixed with fresh fruit juice. This tea will assist digestion and help to stimulate the appetite, aid in settling an upset stomach and help to ease griping stomach pains.

Rosehip
This tea has always been popular for preventing colds because it's an excellent source of vitamin C, as well as vitamins A, E and B.

Drink it hot in winter with a slice of lemon, a little honey and a pinch of spice, or iced in summer with a sprig of spearmint or peppermint, some honey, ice cubes and a slice of lemon.

DRY BATHING

Stimulate circulation and rid your body of accumulated dead cells and toxins by brushing your body with a loofah for five to ten minutes each morning on rising.

Dry bathing consists of brushing all parts of the body below the neck. Women should avoid brushing the delicate breast area and everyone should go very gently and lightly on the paler, softer areas of the stomach and inside areas of the arms and legs. Use gentle yet firm pressure on the rest of the body and brush in a circular motion.

Finish off by gently applying almond or apricot oil all over your body. Leave for ten minutes, then towel off the excess with a vigorous rub.

EARWIGS

These garden pests are brown to reddish-brown in colour and have thick, curved pincers. They come out at night and usually feed on decaying plant material, however they will occasionally make a feast of soft, leafy vegetables, especially if they are beginning to turn brown.

Personally, I don't consider them a problem.

But if they really bother you and are getting into the house, you can make a simple trap to catch them. Firstly, tidy up garden areas close to the house, especially near entrance doors, because earwigs love to hide in mulch, piles of rock, and other debris.

To make a trap, loosely crumple up a piece of newspaper and place it in a suitable container, such as a large tin or planter pot. Sprinkle the paper with water to make it just damp and place two or three of these traps around the garden near mulch and garden rubbish. Check the containers each day around mid-morning and dispose of earwigs and paper.

ENERGY-EFFICIENT HOMES

Today, almost everyone is feeling the energy pinch — the cost of utilities is skyrocketing and increasingly affecting our lives. But we, as individuals, can take an active role in helping to alleviate the problem. By re-evaluating our needs and using energy wisely, we can help to conserve community energy sources. This is especially so in the home where incorporating passive solar design for heating, cooling and partial or full power needs will reduce the drain on non-renewable resources.

SKYLIGHTS

A well-placed skylight can transform an otherwise dark recess of a room into a bright, sunny living area. And not only will you get a view of the sky, your indoor plants will get a new lease on life.

Even a modest 60 cm-square skylight will, on a cloudy day, flood a room with natural light equivalent to three 100 watt light bulbs. If it faces north here in Australia (or south in the northern

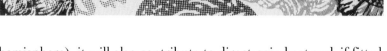

hemisphere), it will also contribute to direct-gain heat and, if fitted with a closable vent, will allow hot air to escape in summer.

There are a number of commercially manufactured skylight units available that can be installed quite easily by the home handyperson. They can be positioned up to 420 cm from the floor without too much loss of light in a location that won't be shaded during winter.

The amount of light gain from the skylight is dependent upon its size and orientation. A good rule of thumb for its size is for its area to be approximately 5 per cent of the floor area to be illuminated. If the room is extremely large, it may be better to have two or three smaller skylights rather than one gigantic one — this will also give you far more even light distribution.

You may wish to have insulated louvres fitted to the skylight to prevent heat from escaping or entering on cold winter nights or hot summer days.

SUNROOM

A glassed-in room, porch or verandah is a simple passive solar system which has tremendous potential. It should face the north (in the southern hemisphere), be attached to rooms like the kitchen, family room and lounge that need daytime heating and be fitted with return and exhaust ventilators. These ventilators should be fitted with shutters to close them off at night, or to be partially closed when the sunroom is used for summer cooling.

Adjustable roof venting will expel the build-up of summer heat and hot air from the house. To operate in summer, close the top inside wall ventilators and open the roof vents. As the air in the sunroom heats, it will be convected through the roof vents and replaced by cooler air from inside the house. By opening south-facing windows (north-facing in the northern hemisphere) or ventilators, cool air will be continually drawn through the house, maintaining a comfortable temperature.

For winter operation, close the roof vents and open both the top and bottom inside ventilators. Keep south-facing windows or ventilators closed. Again, the same principle applies: cooler air is drawn from the house, heated, and instead of being discharged into the atmosphere, redirected into the house.

ATTACHED GREENHOUSE

If you have the room, attaching a greenhouse to an existing wall will provide winter warmth, summer cooling, added living space and somewhere to grow out-of-season vegetables if you're a keen gardener.

Its size depends upon individual needs but, like all solar collectors in the southern hemisphere, it should be attached to a north-facing wall. Include adjustable vents to trap warmth in winter or release summer heat, paint the exterior wall of the house black and install lower and upper ventilators for convective air circulation. Again, inside vents should be shuttered.

Add a verandah or shade house to the south side (north side in the northern hemisphere) of the house to increase the effectiveness of your greenhouse or sunroom for summer cooling. Open adjacent windows or doors during the day — as the air in the greenhouse heats up and is discharged, cool air will be drawn in from outside through doors and windows on the opposite side of the house and will circulate through it. At night, simply close off the greenhouse ventilators until the air warms up from the next day's sunlight.

A greenhouse need not be an expensive, permanent structure. Prefabricated kits are readily available where glass panels simply slot into framework.

It can also serve as a useful winter entrance hall, acting as an air-lock heat trap and reducing the likelihood of cold air entering the house with visitors.

AIR-LOCK HEAT TRAP

Avoid using too many external doors in winter — get into the good habit of using only one. Even better, build a simple foyer or air-lock to prevent warm air escaping and masses of cold air rushing in each time you open the door.

It can be easily constructed from timber framing, lined both sides with plaster-board, and the cavity insulated with natural cellulose fibre. If the foyer is an external addition, match the outside cladding with the outside of the house; insulation is unnecessary. Both doors should be sealed with weatherproof stripping and a draught excluder.

The air-lock will save heat in two ways: there will be minimal heat loss around the doors, and a minimal change of air when entering or leaving the house. But it's important not to have both doors open at the same time, or you'll be defeating the purpose of having the foyer.

Increase the benefits of this structure by installing a few shelves and hooks on one wall for coats, shoes, rainwear or whatever.

SOLAR ELECTRICITY

If you're building a new home, think about solar electricity. It's possible to install a solar system that will provide all your power needs, with the exception of an electric stove, at a cost comparable to what you'll pay for connection to the main power grid. Check out all the costs thoroughly before proceeding, and especially the government cash rebates that are often available for going solar, because they can be quite substantial.

Solar electricity, used in conjunction with standard systems, can be used to cut energy use in existing homes as well. A small solar array and storage batteries can be used to power internal lighting, outdoor lighting, swimming pool filter pumps, internal ceiling fans, exhaust fans and the like, all of which would mean a little less dependence on fossil fuels.

SOLAR HOT WATER

Heating water using solar energy is a sensible, practical and inexpensive way to provide domestic hot water. It's clean, costs nothing to run and requires no maintenance.

The water heater consists of a fixed flat plate absorber, an insulated storage tank and insulated connecting pipes. It works on the 'thermosiphon' principle: warm water rises over colder water. As the water in the absorber heats up, its density decreases, and it rises as heavier cold water pushes it up from beneath, and goes along the transfer pipe to the storage tank. This flow continues until the water fails to gain energy from the sun.

The tank must be situated above the level of the absorber for the system to work. Since the hot water cannot seek a higher level, it is stable in the tank until needed.

Commercially manufactured units are readily available, either with a storage tank mounted directly above the absorber, forming an integral unit, or as two separate components. The latter is far more aesthetically pleasing, as it allows the tank to be mounted in the roof out of sight and can be more effectively insulated.

ESSENTIAL OILS

See Bacteria Busters.

EUCALYPTUS OIL

You'll find a bottle of eucalyptus oil in most households, where the oil will most likely be used as an inhalation to clear stuffy noses. A natural disinfectant, this universal oil has a myriad of other uses around the home. And with more and more people seeking an alternative to products that can be harmful to their health and the environment, all-natural and inexpensive eucalyptus oil is indispensible.

SPOT AND STAIN REMOVAL

Eucalyptus oil will remove spots and stains, including perspiration marks, oil and soluble grease, from clothing. Ideal for work overalls, socks, soiled nappies and sportswear. Simply add 2 teaspoons of oil to each wash load, or use the eucalyptus Wool Mixture below.

Stains can also be removed from fabric by placing an absorbent cloth under the stained area, moistening another cloth with eucalyptus oil, and gently yet firmly brushing towards the centre of the mark.

To remove stains and grease marks from carpet, add eucalyptus oil to a small

spray atomiser and spray generously onto the affected area. Wipe away with a clean absorbent cloth.

Writing ink, printing ink, carbon and other marks can be removed from plastic or vinyl surfaces using a cloth dipped in eucalyptus oil. Test the eucalyptus oil on an unseen area first to check it won't adversely affect the plastic or vinyl.

WOOL MIXTURE

Mix 4 cups of pure soap flakes with 2 cups of methylated spirits and 1 tablespoon of eucalyptus oil. Store in an airtight bottle.

For hand-washing woollens or other clothes, use 1 tablespoon of the mixture in a basin, and proportionately more in the washing machine. Dissolve the mixture in hot water, then add cold water to correct the temperature.

Washing woollens in this mixture will provide protection against moths and silverfish during storage, provided you do not rinse out the eucalyptus oil.

STICKY SUBSTANCE REMOVAL

Eucalyptus oil is excellent for removing substances such as glue, tar, chewing gum and other unknown sticky substances from fabric and other surfaces. Place a few drops of the oil on the stained area, leave for two minutes or until the oil has evaporated, and then wash.

To remove tar from shoes, apply eucalyptus oil, leave for two minutes and sponge off with warm soapy water.

REMOVING ADHESIVE LABELS AND TAPE

Wipe adhesive labels gently with methylated spirits and a few drops of eucalyptus oil to remove from glass or other surfaces.

To remove tape from vinyl surfaces without leaving a mark, moisten well with eucalyptus oil, leave several minutes and lift off. Repeat a few times if necessary, then wipe over with methylated spirits and eucalyptus oil.

DISINFECTANT FLOOR CLEANER

Add 1 teaspoon of eucalyptus oil to the water when washing or mopping over vinyl or linoleum floors.

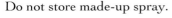

BATHROOM CLEANER

Dissolve 4 ml of eucalyptus oil in 10 ml (2 teaspoons) of methylated spirits. Add to a pump-spray bottle containing 500 ml of water to make a good disinfectant, cleaner and deodorising spray. Shake well to mix and use on a fine mist setting.

This mixture is also excellent for removing mould from ceramic tiles and painted surfaces.

GARDEN SPRAY

Make a safe, non-residual garden spray that's effective against earwigs, slugs, snails and slaters by mixing 1 teaspoon of eucalyptus oil with 500 ml of soapy water. Spray around the base of plants and seedlings and repeat as necessary. Only make up sufficient spray for immediate use and thoroughly wash out the sprayer when finished.

Do not store made-up spray.

MOSQUITO REPELLENT

Dissolve 10 drops of eucalyptus oil in 30 ml of almond oil or any other vegetable oil, and rub well onto exposed skin. Renew every two to four hours.

INSECT BITES

Apply eucalyptus oil to sore and swollen areas for quick relief from the pain of insect bites. Repeat if necessary.

WARM-UP LINIMENT

For a warming, soothing liniment that helps loosen up your muscles before exercise or training, to 20 ml of almond oil add (drop by drop) sufficient eucalyptus oil, ensuring that the mixture remains strongly scented. Massage into the muscle area.

DOG WASH

Add 40 to 60 drops of eucalyptus oil to soapy washing water for a dog wash that reputedly also gets rid of fleas.

Keep flies at bay as well by mixing 1 teaspoon of eucalyptus oil with 1 cup of water and combing this through the animal's fur.

See also Animal Indiscretions.

EXHAUSTION

See Fatigue.

EYE CARE

Eyes are the focal point of your face, and clear, sparkling eyes highlight the glow of a healthy complexion. These delicate mechanisms should be treated with respect — if you have any eye problems, consult your health practitioner immediately and get a referral to an ophthalmologist (eye specialist).

Sleep and relaxation help to keep eyes looking clear and bright, as does a healthy diet. If you haven't been getting enough sleep or if you've been overindulging in alcohol, rich foods or tobacco, the appearance of your eyes will suffer. Follow the tips below to prevent getting tired, strained and bloodshot eyes.

* Take in plenty of vitamin A, which is found in carrots and apricots.
* Bilberry, available from your health-food store as a supplement, will improve the health of your eyes.
* Sleep for eight hours a night as often as possible.
* Refrain from watching too much television.
* Don't read or use your eyes for close work in inadequate light.
* Refresh your eyes with a herbal eyebath (see Eye Lotion, below) if they have been exposed to a smoky atmosphere, salt water or excessive wind and sun.
* Bathe eyes with a soothing and healing herbal wash (see Eye Lotion, below) at the end of each day if you spend long hours working under artificial light.

EYE LOTION

This lotion is ideal for tired, bloodshot and sore eyes.

Put 2 tablespoons of fresh parsley and 1 teaspoon each of dried elderflower and fennel seed in a ceramic bowl. Cover with 300 ml of boiling water, steep until the infusion becomes tepid, then strain through muslin cloth. Bathe eyes in this lotion, using an eyebath (available from pharmacies and supermarkets), when required.

QUICK AND EASY EYE TREATMENTS

If you're feeling tired and your eyelids feel heavy, lie down in a quite, semi-darkened room with your feet raised above the level of your head, and apply any of the treatments that follow.

* Squeeze the excess moisture from tea bags and apply after they have cooled.

* Apply thin slices of raw potato to reduce slight puffiness or a bruised sensation.
* Cooling and soothing slices of cucumber will freshen the eye area and help to keep wrinkles at bay.

DAY-TO-DAY EYE CARE

Because the skin under the eye is very thin and delicate, take care when removing eye make-up. Use a very fine oil, such as apricot or almond, to 'float' the make-up off.

It's important to tone this area after cleansing, to ensure the skin retains its elasticity. Gently pat witch hazel (from pharmacies) on the surrounding eye tissue; avoid applying to much, as this will cause stinging.

EYE SHADOW

See Herbal Make-up.

FABRIC STAINS

See Eucalyptus Oil.

FATIGUE

There are often a number of underlying factors relevant to fatigue, which can include an inadequate diet and in particular an insufficient intake of vitamins and minerals. Lack of the B group vitamins, especially vitamin B_{12}, and the mineral magnesium can cause chronic irritability, a feeling of exhaustion and mental fatigue.

Although supplements are readily available, it is far better to maintain a well-balanced diet which includes fresh fruit and vegetables, and fresh herbs. Foods to help motivate you and get you going are apples, bananas, corn, grapefruit, mangoes, papaya (pawpaw), peaches and yellow squash. A small glass of fresh carrot juice each day is also an excellent boost to the system — of all the juices, it has the best balance of vitamins and minerals.

Natural food sources of magnesium are almonds and other nuts, fish, prawns, leafy green vegetables, molasses, soybeans, sunflower seeds and wheatgerm. Herbs which provide this element are alfalfa (eat daily as sprouted seed), cayenne, dandelion and peppermint. Fresh dandelion leaves can be cooked like spinach or the young, tender leaves chopped up and served in a salad.

Vitamin B group food sources are brewer's yeast (sprinkle over breakfast cereal), grains and seeds (such as wheatgerm), rice bran, sunflower seeds, nuts, legumes, potatoes, almonds, mushrooms, soybeans, citrus fruits, molasses, spinach, cauliflower, salmon, and dairy products such as milk, cheese and whey. Vitamin B_{12} can be found in most meats — which should be eaten as lean cuts, and not in excess. Herb sources of B complex vitamins are dandelion, fenugreek, parsley, alfalfa, watercress, cayenne, burdock and sage.

Include plenty of fresh fruit and vegetables and herbs in your daily diet and you'll probably have the energy to get out and enjoy life, rather than sleeping it away. If the feeling of fatigue persists even though you're eating well, exercising and getting enough sleep, consult your health practitioner.

FERMENT FLIES

See Fruit Fly.

FERTILISER

See Compost Tea, Garden Fertilisers and Green Manuring.

FLATULENCE

Flatulence is usually due to overeating, eating too rapidly or eating unsuitable, hard-to-digest foods. If the problem persists after eliminating these factors and is causing distress, seek professional advice. However, in most circumstances, problems with flatulence can be eased or dispelled by the use of herbs.

The principal herbs for dispelling gas from the stomach and bowels are aniseed, caraway seed, cloves, sweet fennel, ginger, peppermint, thyme and parsley. Drink any of these herbs as a hot herbal tea whenever you suffer from wind.

To make your herbal tea, add 1 teaspoon of dried ground herb to a ceramic cup, add boiling water, cover and steep for three minutes. Strain into another cup and reheat if necessary.

See also Garlic Soup.

FLEA BITE

First bathe the affected areas in an antiseptic made of 1 drop of lavender oil added to one cup of warm water to avoid the risk of infection, then apply undiluted lavender oil. Eucalyptus oil can be used in place of the lavender, or 3 drops of thyme oil diluted in 10 ml (2 teaspoons) of cider vinegar.

FLORAL VINEGAR

For many centuries, aromatic vinegars were used to ward off infection. You can use them as a refreshing and invigorating addition to a hot bath or as an astringent and skin softener. They can also be made into a cooling wash to clean the face and used as a skin toner after cleansing. Floral vinegar also does wonders to freshen up a sick room (see below).

The refreshing quality is due to the acetic acid which dissolves the aromatic substances in herbs and flower petals, making a perfume of a different composition to that made with alcohol.

Aromatic vinegars are best made with a good-quality cider vinegar, and can be scented with petals and herbs such as rose petals, lavender, rosemary, lemon balm, lemon verbena, basil, hyssop, peppermint, scented geranium leaves and jasmine.

Half fill a wide-mouthed, clear glass jar with chopped fresh herbs and top up with warmed vinegar. Seal the jar and leave where it will receive plenty of sunlight for three to four weeks. When ready, strain off the vinegar, squeezing and keeping all the liquid from the herbs, then dilute it by adding an equal amount of distilled water.

If you find it more convenient to use dried herbs or petals to make a floral vinegar, put 3 tablespoons of herbs or 6 tablespoons of petals in a ceramic bowl. Mix together 300 ml each of good-quality cider vinegar and distilled water, and heat to just below boiling point. Pour the liquid over the herbs, cover the bowl tightly with plastic wrap and leave to steep for twelve hours. Strain and bottle for future use.

FACE WASH

2 tablespoons lavender vinegar (see recipe on previous page)
1 cup rose-water

Make a floral vinegar using fresh or dried lavender. Mix with the rose-water and store in tightly capped bottles. Apply directly to face. If lavender isn't the herb of choice for your skin type, use a more suitable herb to create your own astringent vinegar face wash. Use any of the following herbs or flower petals to make your floral vinegar and blend with 1 cup of distilled water.

> *basil (oily and disturbed skin)*
> *honeysuckle (all skin types)*
> *dill (all skin types)*
> *jasmine (sensitive skin)*
> *lemon verbena (oily and disturbed skin)*
> *sweet scented geranium* (Pelargonium peltatum) *leaves*
> *(all skin types)*
> *violet (all skin types)*

FACIAL TONER

Dilute 20 ml of herbal vinegar with 150 ml of distilled water and store in a bottle. Pour a little of this toner onto slightly damp cotton wool, and gently apply to face and neck using outward and upward movements.

IN THE BATH

Add 1 cup of floral vinegar to the bath while the taps are running, or soak a soft face cloth in the vinegar, wring it out and lay it across your forehead while you relax.

REFRESHING A SICK ROOM

Make the surroundings more pleasant for someone confined to bed by soaking a small sponge in lavender vinegar and leaving it in a dish beside the bed.

FLEA REPELLENTS

The family pet is usually the cause of flea infestations, therefore regular control methods are a must. Remember, in ideal conditions it takes just 10 female fleas only 30 days to multiply to a staggering quarter of a million.

Weekly vacuuming of the house and airing of rugs is essential to prevent outbreaks. When vacuuming, do the whole house in a day (not one room a day) and vacuum lounges, cushions, carpets, mats, up and down curtains, along crevices, and beds and their coverings. Take animal bedding, cushions and mats outside and air them in the sun for a day, then vacuum thoroughly before bringing them back inside.

Treat carpets, mats and pet bedding with a flea repellent. Make your own by mixing 18 drops of undiluted pennyroyal oil with 500 grams of bicarbonate soda. Sprinkle over carpets and furniture, leave one hour and vacuum.

Undiluted pennyroyal oil sprinkled over carpets and mats will literally send fleas hopping until they drop from the fumes. But use sparingly — the fumes can be quite overpowering.

Make a flea repellent spray for treating your pet's bedding and places the pet likes to occupy (like lounge cushions) by blending 20 to 30 drops of pennyroyal oil with 10 ml (2 teaspoons) of methylated spirits and then adding the mixture to a pump-spray bottle containing 500 ml of water. Shake well to mix and use on a fine mist setting.

Pennyroyal oil can be purchased from specialty shops that carry essential oils and possibly your local health-food store.

TREATING YOUR PET

Wash pets twice a week with safe, repellent wash if fleas are a problem. Add 30 grams of derris powder (available from garden supply stores) to 5 litres of warm, soapy water and shampoo the animal, massaging the wash well into the fur. Rinse with clean water and apply a repellent lotion of 1 ml of pennyroyal oil diluted in 10 ml (2 teaspoons) of methylated spirits. Apply 20 drops of this lotion to a small animal, such as a kitten, adjusting the quantity according to the size of your pet and taking care not to administer too much, especially in animals under six months old. Start from the tail and work slowly up to the neck, rubbing the lotion through the fur with your fingers. Store the remainder in an airtight, amber-coloured glass bottles for future use.

Rather than purchase a commercial flea collar, dab a few drops of the undiluted pennyroyal oil on a leather collar. Use leather collars for this purpose on both dogs and cats, as leather acts as a natural fixative, preventing rapid evaporation of the oil. Refresh the collar once a week with a few more drops of oil.

You don't need toxic chemicals for successful flea control — a natural approach, combined with careful hygiene and herbal preparations can significantly reduce a potential flea epidemic.

See also Animal Indiscretions (Fleas), Dog Wash and Eucalyptus Oil (Dog Wash).

FLY REPELLENTS

Australia is host to around 200 species of flies, with the major pests being the common housefly and bush fly. Both species begin to annoy us more with the onset of warmer weather and become quite a nuisance if not kept under control.

Houseflies stay close to houses and domestic animal shelters, are most active during the day, and love to shelter indoors. Bush flies are smaller, more annoying and found just about everywhere

in Australia, especially on the inhabitants'
backs and faces.

Keeping these pests at bay can be
extremely trying but there are some
natural remedies worth trying.

HERBS

Many herbs help to deter flies, and can be
grown in the garden or pots close to entry doors and
around patios, verandahs and outdoor entertainment areas.
Choose lavender, sweet woodruff (*Asperula odorata*), lemon
verbena, star anise, tansy, any of the mints, thyme, rosemary, bay,
camomile, garden rue (*Ruta graveolens*), elder, southernwood
(*Artemisia abrotanum*) and basil.

OILS

* Brush pennyroyal oil onto the woodwork surrounding
  doorways and kitchen benches to help keep flies away.
* Tie small muslin bags containing cloves to light fittings.
* Burn eucalyptus, lavender, citronella or peppermint oil in a
  ceramic simmering pot (oil burner) to repel blowflies.
  Simmering pots are available from most gift and novelty shops
  and are designed to sit on dining or coffee tables.
* Add a drop of a repellent essential oil (lavender, citronella,
  peppermint, lemongrass, cinnamon, thyme or basil) to lengths
  of cotton ribbon or strips of paper and hang from the tops of
  window and door frames.

BREEDING GROUNDS

To keep flies, and especially blowflies, from breeding in your
garbage bin, soak strips of old sheeting in a liquid repellent made
by dissolving 10 drops of citronella oil and 3 drops of peppermint
oil in a litre of water. Hang the soaked strips inside the bin.

Check for other possible breeding areas, such as slow compost
heaps, damp bedding in dog kennels, chicken pens and yards,
rubbish piles, and leaking septic pipes and outlets. Ask neighbours
to do likewise.

See also Creepy-crawlies and Insect Pests.

FLY SPRAY

I very seldom use a fly spray, however on the odd occasion when the need has arisen I have had success with the following recipe.

Dissolve 20 ml of eucalyptus oil and 6 ml of bergamot oil in 100 ml of vodka or methylated spirits, then combine with 10 ml of white wine vinegar and 1370 ml of distilled water and mix thoroughly. Store in a pump-spray bottle and use as required.

FOOT CARE

Feet are quite often a neglected part of the body, yet within the average lifetime, they will carry us the equivalent of four times around the world. So take time out and give your feet the attention they deserve.

Most foot problems are caused through a lack of care and badly fitting shoes. This can be avoided by following a few simple guidelines.

* Let your feet breathe — walk barefooted as often as possible to let your feet recover from the confinement of shoes.
* Wear sensible footwear — flat-heeled, comfortable, leather shoes or sandals — whenever possible.
* Shop for shoes in the afternoon, since your feet will swell during the day. And make sure that shoes are at least 2.5 cm longer than the end of your toes.
* Avoid wearing the same pair of shoes every day, and don't buy plastic shoes. Instead, choose leather or fabric that allows the feet to breathe.
* Wear socks made from natural fibres; synthetics will encourage perspiration.
* Sprinkle a little dry, powdered camomile (reduce the camomile to a powder by rubbing through a fine wire sieve) mixed with an equal amount of bicarbonate of soda into shoes after wearing them for the day.
* Give feet a regular pedicure and always cut toenails straight across.
* At the end of a busy day, soak your feet in a soothing footbath. Add 5 drops of essential oil of

thyme and a cup of bicarbonate soda to a
large bowl of warm water. Mix well and soak
your feet for 20 minutes, then massage well
with calendula, thyme or rosemary oil
(12 drops in 10 ml (2 teaspoons) of
an odourless vegetable oil).

* If you don't have time for a separate
foot-bath, rub rosemary oil (diluted
in vegetable oil as above) or apple cider vinegar diluted with
water into your feet, massaging for about five minutes, before
taking a bath.

* To soften dry skin on your feet, wash with a mixture of
1 tablespoon of bran and 3 tablespoons of strong camomile tea
(about 3 level teaspoons of dried camomile steeped in 300 ml
of hot water until cold). Rinse, wipe dry, and moisturise with
hand cream or lotion.

* To soften extra hard skin around the soles of the feet or
the back of the heels, massage in equal quantities of olive oil
and cider vinegar. Keep rubbing until the excess oil is
absorbed.

* Prevent foot odour and excessive perspiration by including
sufficient silica in your diet; eat barley, garlic, onion, parsley,
lettuce and celery. Bathe your feet in a bowl of hot water
containing a few drops of lemongrass oil, then apply a lotion
made by mixing together 18 drops of lemongrass oil and 30 ml
of soya oil. Store in an airtight, amber-coloured glass bottle.

ACHING FEET

Add 2 tablespoons of bicarbonate of soda to a basin of hot water
and soak your feet for at least ten minutes.

For extra sore and aching feet, add 1 tablespoon each of sea salt
and bicarbonate soda to a bowl of hot water, swish around until
completely dissolved then add 3 to 5 drops of rosemary oil. Leave
to cool slightly and then soak your feet.

After ten minutes, revive your feet with a quick dip into a basin
of cold water, and then back into the hot water again. Continue
doing this as long as the salt and sodium bicarbonate water
remains hot.

HERBAL FOOTBATH

Herbs and essential oils are excellent for reviving tired feet. For a comforting and soothing foot bath, add 1 tablespoon of washing soda crystals (available from pharmacies) and 1 to 2 tablespoons of dried herbs or handfuls of fresh ones to a large bowl of boiling water. Choose herbs such as rosemary, comfrey, camomile, lavender, calendula, yarrow, mint, pine needles, sage or scented geranium (*Pelargonium* spp.) leaves — any or all of them.

Pack the herbs loosely in a thin muslin bag and tie with a piece of ribbon before immersing them in the water if you want to reduce the mess factor.

Cover the bowl and allow the herbs to steep for 30 minutes. Remove the herbs and bring the liquid to the boil in a stainless steel or enamel pan. Return herbal water to the bowl, allow to cool until it feels comfortable, and then soak your feet. After ten minutes revive your feet with a quick dip into a basin of cold water, and then back again into the footbath. Continue doing this as long as the herb water remains hot, then finish off with a cold dip.

A tablespoon of sea salt can be added to the water if your feet are extremely tired or sore.

If it has been raining and you have cold, wet feet, a pinch or two of mustard powder added to the water is invigorating.

Finish off by massaging your feet with a soothing herbal lotion made by blending together 6 drops of rosemary oil, 15 ml of almond oil and 5 ml of avocado oil in a small, amber-coloured glass bottle. Store any remaining lotion in a cool, dark cupboard.

See also Fungicide.

FRAGRANCE

The refreshing and aromatic properties of herbs and flowers can be used in many different ways to keep your home smelling fragrant and fresh. They will remove stale and other unwanted odours, freshen up cupboards and drawers, add a soothing drift of scent in the bedroom and give your linen and clothes a touch of fragrant luxury.

Fragrant Wash

To add a delightful fragrance to your wash, put 3 to 5 drops of lemongrass or lavender oil onto a face washer and include it in the final rinse. If hand-washing, include 2 drops of a chosen oil in the final rinse and swish it around. For a more exotic scent, try ylang-ylang or neroli.

Sweet-smelling Rooms

Keep rooms smelling fresh and eliminate bad odours with an aromatic air-freshener spray. Dissolve 25 drops each of lavender and lemon oils and 10 drops of geranium oil in 10 ml of methylated spirits and blend with 500 ml of water. Store in a pump-spray bottle and use as required.

Clean-smelling Kitchens

When washing out the fridge, freezer or oven, add a drop of lemon or bergamot oil to the final rinse water. This will deodorise without permeating the fridge or other surfaces with an aroma.

For wiping over surfaces such as the kitchen benchtop, sink, tiles or paintwork, add 1 drop of lavender, lemon or eucalyptus oil directly to the cloth or include 7 drops of oil in the rinse water.

Cupboards and Drawers

Add 2 to 3 drops of lavender or lemon oil to cotton-wool balls and place them in cupboards and drawers. To keep moths away from clothes, add lavender, lemongrass, camphor or rosemary oil to cotton-wool balls and place them between the clothes.

Burning Essential Oils

Burning essential oils in a simmering pot (oil burner) will kill airborne bacteria and fungi. Try thyme, lavender, pine or eucalyptus for their fresh fragrance.

A simmering pot is a small ceramic vessel with a candle inside. A saucer containing a mixture of essential oil and water sits on top and the burning candle releases its fragrant vapours. Add about 10 drops of essential oil to 1 cup of boiling water, preheat the saucer by lighting and burning the candle for a while, and then three-quarters fill the saucer with the fragrant water, topping up when required.

FRUIT FLY

The home garden and orchard, no matter how humble, can provide fresh fruit and vegetables, and a place to escape from the rigours of daily life. It can also become a battleground as you try to combat the many unwanted pests that invade it, greedily devouring everything in sight.

The fruit fly is one pest that can, if left unchecked, become a serious problem and have devastating effects. However it can be kept under control with easy-to-make traps, using no more than recyclable materials.

In my plum orchard I make traps from empty plastic ice-cream containers. Cut a hole about 25 mm in diameter in two opposite sides, a little over halfway up. Next make 6 to 8 holes about 6 mm in diameter in the lid.

Fill each container 1 to 2 cm below the side holes with a strong sugar and soapy water solution. (The soapy water breaks the water tension so that the flies drown more easily.) Add a piece of banana skin, secure the lid with masking tape, and hang the container in a harness made from string in a shady part of the tree away from direct sunlight. Place 1 to 3 traps in each tree, depending upon its size.

This type of trap is extremely effective and will need to be emptied and recharged once a week.

In addition to your traps, you must never leave fruit to rot on the ground. Pick up fallen fruit daily, and if you keep ducks or chickens, allow them to free range near your trees.

The vegetable garden can also function as an ideal maternity ward for this pest, especially with plants such as tomatoes. You can make smaller traps from empty jam jars and hang them strategically throughout the garden. Pierce a hole about thumbnail size in the jar's lid and add the bait.

Check the traps every second day and empty if necessary, as they may have to be recharged more frequently than the larger ice-cream container variety.

Ferment flies, which are found indoors and sometimes mistaken for fruit fly, can be controlled with the same type of trap if their activities really bother you. A far simpler solution is to keep over-ripe fruit covered.

FUNGICIDE

Make an all-purpose household fungicide by blending 1 part tea tree oil to 10 parts water. Suitable for use in the bathroom and for applying to your feet to treat tinea.

FURNITURE POLISH

See Cleaners, Jasmine Furniture Polish and Polish.

GARDEN FERTILISERS

LIQUID COMFREY

Comfrey is a green, leafy herb available from most nurseries and is easily grown in the backyard garden. Its leaves make a thick, green, pungent liquid manure that can be used for all garden plants, and is especially good for promoting rapid growth in vegetables.

To make the fertiliser, pick fresh comfrey leaves and half-fill a large bucket, preferably one with a lid, or a large plastic garbage bin, then fill with water. Leave to steep for three months then dilute 1 part comfrey compost to 2 parts water before sprinkling around plants.

COUCH GRASS FERTILISER

Couch grass makes a good liquid fertiliser. See the instructions for making and use as for liquid comfrey, above.

SEAWEED FERTILISER

If you're lucky enough to live near the ocean, seaweed can be used to make a spray-on fertiliser that also doubles as a natural fungicide for vegetables, ornamentals and trees.

Gather sufficient seaweed to fill one-fifth of a drum or large garbage bin, rinsing away thoroughly all traces of salt before putting it into the drum or bin. Cover with water and allow to steep for three weeks, then dilute with 2 parts of fresh water. Spray onto foliage of plants or apply at soil level.

When the concentrate is exhausted, the seaweed can be used as a mulch or added to your compost.

See also Compost Tea and Green Manuring.

GARDEN SENSE

Australians are known for their love of the outdoors, so it's only natural that gardens form an important part of most people's lives. Among other things, the garden provides a personal oasis to relax and unwind from work, and also becomes a centre for family entertainment. Here are some hints on how to maintain this oasis.

NATURAL DEFENCE MECHANISMS

With the onset of spring and warmer weather, gardens begin to shed their winter coats and display magnificent colour. But spring is also a time when gardens are often besieged by a multitude of different insects eager to feast on young seedlings. Rather than reaching for a chemical spray that's guaranteed to murder the insects — along with everything else that lives in the garden — develop a healthy environmental attitude. Work with Nature to create a garden environment where plants and trees thrive without the use of poisonous pesticides.

The wise use of mulching, the careful selection of ground-cover plants, hand-weeding, companion planting with herbs and mixed plantings instead of monoculture are safer.

Make use of natural predators. Your garden is literally teeming with living creatures all of which create a balance that provides for a healthy garden. And plagues only occur when the natural balance is upset.

Some natural predators are easy to see: ladybirds kill aphids; native snails (*Strangesta*) kill common garden snails; and birds and spiders eat lots of insects.

Try picking pests off by hand, learn about their life cycles and attempt to reduce their numbers when they are least active. Encourage friendly species of insects and other creatures to live in your garden and feed on those you wish to eradicate. Frogs, beetles, bees, praying mantis and lizards are also predators of common garden pests and will help to maintain an ideal ecological balance.

Plant herbs and vegetables together to repel insect attack and to promote the growth and flavour of your vegetables. Marigolds, rosemary, onions, garlic, lavender, peppermint and chives are among the strong-smelling flowers and herbs that repel insects and can be interspersed among the other plants to do just that.

THE WELL-FED AND WELL-KEPT GARDEN

Mulching your garden with organic matter, such as home-made compost, manure (cow or horse are the best choice and should be

pulverised before adding to the soil), grass clippings and pine-bark chips, is one of the best and most efficient ways of keeping soil and plants healthy and happy. And apart from improving soil texture, mulching will reduce the need for excessive watering, keep the soil moist and prevent moisture loss through evaporation, which is especially important in drought-affected areas and a useful practice for us all as we try to conserve water.

Keep your garden free of weeds, rank grass, fallen fruit from fruit trees, diseased plants, piles of rotting timber and sheets of iron. This will reduce the habitat for garden pests and help maintain garden hygiene.

If you find you need to spray, do so only as a last resort, and always use an organic spray.

ORGANIC SPRAY

A suitable all-purpose spray can be made by mixing in a blender half a cup of garlic, 4 hot chilli peppers and 1 litre of soapy water. Before use, dilute 1 part of this concentrate with 10 parts of water and spray as required, but only in the late afternoon when all bee activity has ceased.

PEST CONTROL WITHOUT PESTICIDES

Start by having healthy plants, as they are highly resistant to insect, fungal or bacterial attack. Next, take advantage of the natural insect repellent qualities of some herbs and plants: marigolds kill root-destroying nematodes; garlic repels aphids and many flying insects; misty plume bush (*Iboza brevispicata*) or river plume bush (*Iboza riparia*) planted near the kitchen door will discourage houseflies. Try planting other insect-repellent Australian natives, such as prosantheras. Find plants in their native habitat and observe their insect-repelling qualities.

Remember, insect repellent plants will discourage rather than completely eliminate the pest, so be prepared to accept some plant losses.

Grow herbs for their pest-repellent qualities as well as for cooking and medicine. Basil will repel houseflies and fruit flies. Elderflower deters flies; rub the leaves on your skin. Mint repels ants, flies and black beetles, and rosemary repels carrot fly and

cabbage and house moths. Plant tansy near the house to repel fleas, ants, flies and moths, and thyme will repel cabbage root fly.

The Right Plants in the Right Place

Plant extra fruit and vegetables to allow for some natural loss. And when your favourite plant becomes ill, question its suitability to the location before rushing out to buy poisons. Particularly with native plants, you may have face some failures until you find plants that really suit your land.

Companion Planting

Don't grow plants together that aren't compatible. Here are some successful combinations: grow borage with strawberries; dill with corn and celery; parsley with roses; asparagus with tomatoes; basil with tomatoes; peas with corn, radishes, beans, cucumber and carrots; and lettuce with carrots. Avoid putting garlic and onions near beans and peas. And tomatoes and pumpkins don't go well near potatoes.

Mineral Deficiencies

If plants are growing poorly, being attacked by insect pests, or are disease-prone, it's a fairly good indication of deficiencies. In most cases these deficiencies can be corrected by the addition of lots of organic matter to the soil, or sometimes the problem can be solved by adjusting the pH (acidity or alkalinity) level. Refer to the following list to identify and correct any mineral deficiencies.

Nitrogen
SIGNS: slender fibrous stems, foliage and stems fade from green to yellow and the plant's growth tends to slow down.
SOLUTION: add plenty of well-rotted poultry manure, which has a very high nitrogen content; other good sources of nitrogen are compost, blood and bone, and fish scraps.

Phosphorous
SIGNS: growth slows down, the underside of leaves turn reddish-purple; fruit trees may lose their fruit early or set fruit late.
SOLUTION: add lots of manure, compost and other organic matter.

Potassium

SIGNS: plants grow poorly, leaves turn bronze-coloured and curl up; root systems are underdeveloped.

SOLUTION: make a separate compost heap that contains plenty of stable manure and green matter, plus wood ash if you can get it; spread this compost over the surface of the soil and keep well mulched with organic matter.

Boron

SIGNS: slow growth is evident; plants become bushy and the terminal buds die; later, the lateral buds die, the roots or tubers crack and the leaves thicken.

SOLUTION: mulch with well-rotted manure or compost.

Calcium

SIGNS: thick, woody stems and retarded growth, blackening and dying of roots; in some instances, terminal buds and young branches may be deformed.

SOLUTION: treat with ground natural limestone.

Copper

SIGNS: slow growth, shoots and tips die back — this is especially evident in fruit trees.

SOLUTION: apply plenty of compost or well-rotted manure; adding rock minerals can also be helpful (they can be included in the compost heap).

Iron

SIGNS: top leaves turn yellow, young foliage has spotted and coloured areas.

SOLUTION: avoid over-liming; add plenty of well-rotted manure, crop residues (what is left over after harvesting a crop), and blood and bone.

Magnesium

SIGNS: growth is very slow and plants are late to mature; the entire leaf can become mottled with dead areas, and the spaces between veins on older leaves may turn yellow; on fruit trees, watch for patches of dead tissue on older leaves, or leaves dropping — first on old branches, then twigs from current season.

SOLUTION: add seaweed to your compost heap, or a litre of sea water to every 50 kg of compost; incorporate dolomite directly into the soil or include some in your compost pile.

Zinc

SIGNS: leaves may become mottled, turn yellow, and become abnormally long and narrow; this can be a problem in peat soils.

SOLUTION: incorporate plenty of well-rotted manure and raw phosphate rock minerals, if you can get them.

See also Compost Tea, Eucalyptus Oil, Garden Fertilisers, Garden Spray and Green Manuring.

GARDEN SPRAY

This is particularly effective against scale, thrips, mites and aphids.

Place 3 chopped onions, 4 chopped garlic cloves, 2 tablespoons of cayenne pepper and 500 ml of water in a blender. Blend at high speed until liquified.

Dissolve 1 tablespoon of grated, pure soap (or soap flakes) in 500 ml of water and mix with the onion and garlic liquid. Store in a tightly sealed glass bottle, label and keep out of reach of children.

See also Compost Tea, Eucalyptus Oil and Garden Sense.

GARLIC SOUP

The more red meat you eat, the more you need a good amino acid balance. Although red meat does contain these acids, the digestive tract may not be in a clean enough state to adequately cope with the digestion and easy assimilation of the proteins in meat. This causes stomach rumblings and production of offensive antisocial gases.

To avoid this problem, it is important to include natural sources of sulphur in your diet — avocados, celery, cucumber, mushrooms, tomatoes, onions (all types) and garlic.

Garlic is especially useful for cleansing toxins from your bloodstream, as well as aiding in digestion and cleansing stale mucus from your tissues. And taken on a regular basis, it will help your body build resistance to winter colds and relieve the symptoms of sinusitis.

In my family, the favourite way of enjoying and taking advantage of the many benefits of garlic is by eating my grand-mother's garlic soup.

> *8 cloves of fresh garlic*
> *2 large new potatoes, skins on (pontiacs are best)*
> *3 to 4 cups of water*
> *1 bay leaf*
> *a few sprigs of fresh sage*
> *a few sprigs of fresh thyme*
> *salt substitute (see Salt Substitute)*
> *freshly ground black pepper*

Peel the garlic cloves and cut the potatoes into small chunks. Put both in a saucepan, add water and bay leaf, cover and cook for fifteen minutes. Cool, then add finely cut fresh herbs. Sieve or blend the soup. Season and reheat to serve.

The flavour of this soup increases the day after it is made. Although the flavour can't be compared, dried herbs can be substituted for fresh ones.

GREASE STAINS

Whether you're buying or eating takeaway food or doing an oil change on your car to save money, grease stains are inevitable. They can ruin clothes, velour car seat covers and, if the grease is tracked into the house, carpet and furniture coverings, and an oil leak from a car will leave unsightly stains on a driveway.

But you can remove grease stains effectively without having to resort to using harsh chemicals. All you need is items commonly found in the home or supermarket.

CLOTHING

To remove grease from clothes and work overalls, soak the stained area in methylated spirits, then wash, adding 1 tablespoon of the

following eucalyptus and borax wash to every 9 litres of water in your washing machine.

EUCALYPTUS AND BORAX WASH

Blend 450 grams of grated pure soap or soap flakes with 50 grams of purified borax (available from pharmacies and health-food stores) and melt in a double saucepan over a gentle heat, stirring constantly. Pour into an empty milk carton and allow to cool and harden, then reduce again to flakes — running the soap over an inverted carpenter's plane is the quickest and easiest way to do this. Alternatively, you could use a cheese grater, but this method will take a little longer.

Add the soap and 60 ml of methylated spirits to a large glass jar and allow to stand overnight, then add 1 tablespoon of eucalyptus oil. Store until needed, giving a good shake before use.

Grease, oil and fat can also be removed by pouring boiling water over the grease spot, then dusting liberally with bicarbonate of soda and working it thoroughly into the stain. Follow by washing the garment normally.

VELOUR SEAT COVERS

To remove takeaway food grease, smother with a thick layer of talcum powder, place a towel over the powder and hold a hot iron on the towel until the grease comes up into the powder. Be careful not to touch the synthetic velour fabric with the iron, as it will probably melt. Any remaining stain can be sponged with a little of the eucalyptus and borax wash (described above) dissolved in some warm water.

CARPET

Grease and oil stains can be removed from woollen carpet using a thick paste made from water and kaolin (also known as China clay, and available from pharmacies). Spread this paste over the soiled area and leave until completely dry — usually about 24 to 36 hours. After this time, reduce to a powder using a stiff broom, then vacuum up.

Rub any faint residue with a rag dipped in natural turpentine, working from the outside to the centre.

DRIVEWAYS

Oil stains and grease can be removed from concrete driveways by first covering with diatomaceous earth — a readily available source of this absorbent material is kitty litter. Leave on for four to five hours, then sweep up. Any residual stain can be removed with a solution of 1 part biodegradable detergent to 6 parts kerosene.

See also Eucalyptus Oil.

GREEN MANURING

Deficient soils can be improved by planting green manure crops, such as lupins and cowpeas. They benefit the soil by improving the physical condition or crumb structure, conserving mineral matter and increasing nitrogen content, improving drainage and temporarily increasing the quantity of organic matter.

A green manure crop is a means of providing a source of readily available plant food, which benefits succeeding crops by the fertilising ingredients contained in the decaying mass of vegetation.

The process simply involves growing the appropriate crop, allowing top growth to develop, slashing it down and then digging it into the soil to rot. However, success depends upon conditions favourable to the decomposition of the buried material: sufficient warmth and moisture. The more immature the crop, and the lighter textured and aerated the soil, the more rapidly the nutrients will be released.

Green manure crops can be sown at any time there is ample water. Though it is best to grow crops suited to their season, New Zealand blue lupins, field peas or vetches can be sown in autumn; in spring and early summer, cowpeas and Japanese millet, alone or in combination, are good green manure crops.

Broadcast 200 grams of lupin and field pea seeds per 8 square metres, and 125 grams of vetch, cowpea and Japanese millet seed per 8 square metres. Sow the seed on prepared moist soil and cover to a depth of 2 to 5 cm.

After digging in, sow the next crop of green manure or garden plants immediately, taking care not to place seeds or seedlings in a pocket of chopped-up material.

See also Garden Fertilisers and Compost Tea.

HAEMORRHOIDS

See Borage.

HAND CARE

Our hands can suffer from the rigours of day-to-day living. They're affected by wind, the sun, hot and cold weather, harsh cleaning agents and the many tasks they're used to perform daily. This causes the skin to become dry and scaly or, in severe cases, chapped and split.

As well as taking advantage of the natural protection offered by herbal softeners and moisturisers, keep your hands in top condition by following these golden rules:

* Always apply a protective barrier cream before commencing rough work, washing dishes or messy household jobs.
* Wear protective gloves for gardening and household chores as often as possible.
* Avoid direct contact with chemical cleansers or, better still, use only products that are kind to both your skin and the environment.
* Moisturise your hands morning and night, and immediately after any rough work or contact with water.
* Clean ingrained dirt and stains from your hands by dipping them in warm almond oil, then rubbing them with a mixture of coarse sea salt and equal amounts of dried camomile, sage and yarrow — enough to form a paste. This mixture is great for cleaning hands after a session in the garden.
* Keep a small bowl of fine bran near the kitchen sink or laundry tub. Instead of using soap, which can be very drying if used too often, dip your hands in the bran and rub thoroughly to cleanse them, then rinse off.
* If your hands are very dry, soak them for half an hour in warm almond oil with 2 drops of carrot oil added.
* Strengthen your fingernails by soaking them in a bowl of water to which 1 tablespoon of cider vinegar has been added.
* Clean nicotine and other stains from your fingernails by applying lemon juice with a small paintbrush twice a day.

HAND-FRIENDLY ESSENTIAL OILS

Soak your hands for ten minutes each day in a bowl of warm water to which healing or therapeutic oils have been added to keep them in good condition. Add 2 to 4 drops of any of the following oils to a basin of warm water.

Dry Hands
Use rose, geranium or carrot.

Neglected Hands
Use rose, geranium, lemon.

After soaking, massage in a generous amount of hand lotion made of equal quantities of lemon juice, glycerine and rose-water, not forgetting to include your wrists.

Store remaining lotion in an airtight, amber-coloured glass bottle.

HAIR

See Dandruff and Herbal Hair Care.

HAIR SPRAY

A simple hair spray can be made by dissolving a heaped teaspoon of gelatin in a cup of boiling water, and adding a teaspoon of sugar and a few drops of your favourite fragrant oil. Stir until the gelatin melts, cool and store in a pump-spray bottle.

HANGOVER

Drinking plenty of fresh lemon juice in water or freshly squeezed orange juice for extra vitamin C, or hot peppermint or thyme tea, can alleviate the discomfort of a hangover. A herbal tea of equal parts of yarrow and elderflower will also help to eliminate toxins from the body.

See also Xmas (Overindulgence).

HATS

FELT
General Cleaning
Pack the crown of the hat with
paper so that it retains its shape
until no longer damp.

Mix together 360 grams (4 cups) pure soap flakes, 500 ml
(2 cups) methylated spirits and 1 tablespoon of eucalyptus oil.

Dissolve 1 tablespoon of this eucalyptus wash (store remainder
in an airtight bottle) in a basin of hot water, then adjust the water
temperature until tepid. Ring out a rough towel in the solution and
sponge the dirty areas.

Greasy Marks
These are usually caused by the oils from
your hair and are found on the inside of
the band. Simply smother them with
talcum powder or powdered kaolin
(China clay — available from
pharmacies and ceramic suppliers) and
dust off when the grease is absorbed.

Perspiration Stains
Rub with eucalyptus oil or sponge with eucalyptus wash
(see General Cleaning, above).

Water Marks
Sponge with white vinegar.

STRAW
Do not use water on a straw hat as the result will be disastrous,
causing it to lose its shape. Instead, make a cleaning powder by
mixing together equal amounts of powdered borax (available from
pharmacies and health-food stores), salt and
powdered kalolin (China clay —
available from pharmacies or
ceramic suppliers) with just
sufficient eucalyptus oil to form
a stiff powder. Pack over soiled

areas, leave for an hour, then brush off. Repeat the procedure if necessary for really bad stains or dirty marks.

HAY FEVER

Hay fever is triggered by things like house dust, foods, feathers, industrial fumes and polluted air.

Herbal solutions have been used for centuries to provide relief from both hay fever and sinusitis. Garlic and Echinacea provide antimicrobial support to keep the many bugs that flourish in our mucus-filled sinuses under control. Horseradish helps to remove mucus from the nasal and sinus passages, while fenugreek helps soothe irritated nasal and sinus tissues, and also helps to dry up the catarrh allergy sufferers are prone to.

Herbs for hay fever and sinusitis relief are available in supplement form from health-food stores. For watery and itchy eyes, congested sinuses and a runny nose, look for a sinus and catarrh complex containing horseradish and garlic.

INHALANT REMEDY

Add 3 drops of rosemary oil and 1 drop each of thyme and peppermint oils to a bowl of boiling water. Lean over the bowl, cover your head with a large towel to form a tent and inhale the vapour for approximately ten minutes each evening. People prone to high blood pressure, heart problems and sensitive or broken skin should avoid this treatment unless advised otherwise by a health practitioner.

For a convenient inhalant you can be used anywhere, blend together 2 drops of rosemary oil and 1 drop each of geranium and eucalyptus oils. Put 1 drop on a tissue or handkerchief and inhale whenever needed to ease laboured breathing and a stuffy nose.

HERBAL BATHS

Long before we had the high-tech research into cosmetics that we have today, men and women devised simple health and beauty remedies using herbs. And one of the simplest ways to enjoy a herbal beauty treatment is in the bath. All you have to do is tie up a handful of selected herbs in a square of muslin and either hang it from the tap, so that the water gushes through it while you fill the tub, or place it in the bath itself to soak in the water.

Mint, rosemary and lavender are used to stimulate circulation, revitalise the skin and energise the body. Lavender also gives off a marvellous fragrance.

Camomile and thyme will soothe, soften and calm the skin, while comfrey will heal chapped, sore and blemished skin.

Include bay leaf, hyssop and rosemary to ease tired and aching muscles after a strenuous workout.

To cleanse the skin and make it feel smooth, add 2 tablespoons of medium ground oatmeal to your herbs. When the water is sufficiently scented, use the herb bag to scrub your body, paying particular attention to heels, knees and elbows. Oatmeal is a well-known skin softener, and you'll actually feel like the impurities and rough skin are floating away.

HERBAL BATH OIL

There's a huge variety of commercial bath products available, but it's far more rewarding to make your own oils out of pure and natural ingredients.

To make your bath oil, dilute 50 drops of your chosen oil or oil combination and 5 ml of wheatgerm oil in 45 ml of almond oil. Store in an airtight amber-coloured glass bottle away from heat and direct sunlight.

Add 10 drops of this oil mixture while the water is running from the taps, then swish it around before getting into the bath.

NOURISHING BATH OIL

Dilute 40 drops of rose oil and 10 drops of lavender oil in 10 ml of avocado oil, 10 ml of wheatgerm oil and 30 ml of almond oil. Put this oil blend in a dark-coloured airtight bottle and shake well until thoroughly mixed.

Add a teaspoon to your bath water to nourish, soften and moisturise your skin.

See also Lavender (Lavender Bath Water).

HERBAL DRINKS

See Dandyade, Drinks, Indigestion, Nettle and Sleep.

HERBAL HAIR CARE

Beautifully clean, bouncy, shiny hair is an enviable asset. The condition of your hair is usually a fair indication of the state of your general health, so to maintain your hair's good looks you must also maintain all-round good health. It's surprising how quickly your hair will lose its sheen and body when you're feeling slightly out of sorts.

Maintaining a healthy, balanced diet is essential, because your hair needs the B vitamin complex, vitamin A, calcium, silica, iron, zinc, protein and unsaturated oils or fatty acids. Eat plenty of fresh fruit, vegetables and salads, drink lots of water and make sure you get enough sleep — eight hours rest each night will do wonders for your hair.

Although diet is the foundation of healthy hair, herbs will also help to bring out its natural beauty. Their gentle cleansing and conditioning action will leave hair shiny and manageable.

Those old-fashioned tips from grandma's day, like shampooing with an egg to bring life to dry hair and using a lemon juice or vinegar rinse for oily hair, still work. Similarly, traditional herbal rinses made from rosemary, nettle or yarrow massaged into the scalp after shampooing will stimulate hair growth and help control dandruff and over-active sebaceous glands.

To nourish your hair and keep it looking shiny and healthy, use the following quick and easy weekly treatment.

Put 20 ml of almond oil, 20 ml of wheatgerm oil, 20 ml of glycerin, 10 ml of cider vinegar, 3 drops each of rosemary and carrot oils, and 2 eggs into a ceramic bowl. Beat vigorously until thoroughly mixed. After shampooing, apply the mixture, working it well into the hair, then cover with a shower cap. Leave for 20 minutes, then shampoo out using lukewarm water — don't use hot water or you'll scramble the egg. To finish, use the following rosemary hair rinse, which will help revitalise the scalp and hair and will also help prevent dandruff.

Put 6 fresh, leafy rosemary stalks (or 2 tablespoons of dried rosemary) in an enamel or stainless steel saucepan, add 5 cups of distilled water and bring to the boil. Reduce heat and simmer for 30 minutes, keeping the lid on so that the vapour does not escape. Remove from the heat, steep until cold and strain through muslin.

Thoroughly rinse out all traces of shampoo with clean water, then massage the rosemary lotion well into your scalp with your fingertips.

See also Dandruff, Hair Spray and Kids.

HERBAL MAKE-UP

It would be virtually impossible to reproduce the vast colour range of commercially available cosmetic products at home, but it is possible to make a few preparations that will satisfy your basic needs adequately.

LIP GLOSS

> *1 teaspoon of alkanet root*
> *15 g of beeswax*
> *60 ml of almond oil*
> *3 drops of tincture of benzoin*

Crush the alkanet root and place it in a glass jar. Warm the almond oil, add it to the jar and seal tightly. Place where it will receive plenty of sunlight for 14 days. Strain the oil and set aside.

After this 14-day period, melt the beeswax in a double saucepan over a gentle heat. When completely liquid, stir in the warmed alkanet oil, remove from heat, add tincture of benzoin and beat continuously until cool and creamy. Store in a sterilised glass jar.

LIPSTICK

> *2 tablespoons of alkanet root*
> *30 g of beeswax*
> *120 ml of sesame oil*
> *3 drops of tincture of benzoin*

Prepare as for lip gloss. When the mixture has set hard, pour it into a sterilised glass jar or empty lipstick containers.

EYE SHADOW

> *120 ml of almond oil*
> *30 g of beeswax*
> *30 g of selected herb or flower for colouring*
> *3 drops of tincture of benzoin*

Gently simmer the selected herb or flower in the almond oil until its dye has been released. Remove from heat, cool, and strain through clean muslin.

Melt the beeswax in a double saucepan over a low heat. When completely liquid, add the herb oil, mixing thoroughly, then remove from heat. Add tincture of benzoin and beat continuously until cool. Store in a cool, sterilised glass jar.

Use any of the following herbs to colour your eye shadow:

HERB	PART USED	COLOUR
Alkanet	root	soft pink-brown
Blackberry	young shoots	creamy fawn
Camomile *(dyers)* *	flowers	bright yellow
Elder	berries	purple
Juniper	dried berries	olive brown
Lady's bedstraw *(Galium cruciata)*	roots	coral pink
Madder *(Rubia tinctorum)*	roots	rich tomato red
Marigold *(Calendula)*	petals	pale yellow
Onion	skins	orange
Parsley	leaves and stems	cream
Privet	berries	bluish-green
Safflower	flowers	beige
Sorrel	roots	soft pink
Turmeric	powdered root	gold-orange
Walnut	leaves	creamy fawn
Walnut	green husks and shells	shades of brown
Wild marjoram	leaves	violet

* A type of camomile known for its strong colour.

You can also use beetroot, blackcurrant, and black or blue malva flowers. Alternatively, you can experiment with other plants to see what colours they will produce.

HERBAL SKIN CARE

Since early times, human beings have used plant extracts to enhance their appearance and have included them in products to take care of their skin. Ancient and primitive tribes used these plants, often combined with different earths, to colour and decorate their faces and bodies. Cleopatra bathed in asses' milk to keep herself beautiful and Venetian women dyed their hair with saffron and henna for golden or auburn curls.

For many centuries, these simple substances and herbs were the only source of cosmetics, and remained so until cheaper-to-produce synthetic substances gradually replaced them.

Some herbs were chosen for their special properties. An extract of yarrow was used to suppress skin inflammations, aid skin cleansing and remove dead skin cells. Camomile was used as a soothing agent, while calendula (marigold) oil was used to clean and soften the skin, and soothe irritation.

One of the most loved and widely used herbs was rosemary. It was included in skin tonics because of its astringent qualities and became a principal ingredient in shampoos and hair rinses.

Folklore also influenced the choice of herbs used. Bay leaf, for example, was thought to ward off evil. Yet, in spite of such beliefs, the remarkable cosmetic potency of herbs was also recognised.

Once again, people have begun to realise the importance of the natural benefits obtained from using plants and herbs. And, in most cases, the preparation of plants and herbs for skin care purposes is quite easy.

STRAWBERRY SKIN REVITALISER

An old beauty treatment for refreshing and revitalising the skin can be made quickly and simply from nothing more than fresh strawberries.

Cut up and mash to a pulp enough strawberries to spread all over the face and neck. Cleanse your face and neck and apply the pulp, avoiding the eye area. Lie down and relax for 20 minutes while the facial mask does its work. For extra benefit, soak cotton-wool balls in cold fennel tea and place them over your closed eyelids.

Rinse the mask off with warm water, then splash cold water all over the face and neck and pat dry with a soft towel.

ROSE-WATER REJUVENATING LOTION

To make a soothing and rejuvenating skin lotion, warm a cup of clear honey in a saucepan, then add half a cup of milk and 2 teaspoons of rose-water, turning off the heat as you do. Stir the mixture thoroughly, allow to cool, then pour into a sterilised container and store in the refrigerator.

Before using, stir well and then pour a little of the lotion into a saucer. Soak cotton-wool balls in the lotion and pat onto the face and neck every night. Do not rinse off until the following morning.

See also Arms, Cucumber Cold Cream, Jojoba Cleansing Oil and Jojoba Moisturising Lotion, Lavender (Lavender Bath Water), Legs and Skin.

HERBAL SOAP

There is no doubt that people in our society are becoming more 'herb-minded'. They now realise the benefits of using Nature's ingredients for a host of beneficial products, from cleaning the house to cleaning themselves. And what better way to use herbs than to include them in your own custom-made soaps?

A good herbal soap has an effect on the outer layer of the skin — the so-called horny or epithelial layer — making it smooth and soft. You can make your special soaps by saving leftover soap scraps and using them, or using a grated, pure toilet soap.

CAMOMILE SOAP

Soothing and healing camomile soap is suitable for all skin types, including inflamed or irritated skin. It is ideal for men whose facial skin suffers trauma from daily shaving.

86

Put 5 tablespoons of dried camomile flowers in a ceramic bowl and pour 300 ml of boiling water over them. Cover and infuse for twelve hours. Strain through muslin, squeezing and keeping all the liquid from the herbs.

Melt 350 grams of grated soap in an enamel pan over a low heat with just enough of the camomile infusion to form a soft paste (use a potato masher to help dissolve the soap). Add the remaining infusion and stir continuously until thoroughly blended. Remove from heat and pour into suitable moulds. Allow to harden, remove from moulds, and your soap is ready to use.

Moulds for the soap mixture can be small, and shallow cardboard boxes, patty pans, chocolate moulds, clean milk cartons — anything you can think of. And you can increase the quantity of the recipe, proportionately, to make more soap.

HONEY SOAP

This soap is very gentle and particularly suitable for dry and sensitive skin.

Put 2 teaspoons of dried elderflower in a ceramic bowl and pour 300 ml of boiling water over it. Cover, infuse and strain as for the camomile infusion, above. Put 900 grams of grated soap in the top of a double boiler with barely enough hot elderflower infusion to cover. Melt over boiling water, stirring thoroughly, and add 110 grams each of almond oil and clear honey. Continue to stir for ten minutes, mixing well. Remove from heat and pour into moulds to cool. Allow to harden and it's ready for use.

HERBAL STEEL WOOL

See Horsetail.

HERBAL TEA

See Drinks, Indigestion and Sleep.

HERBS

See *Dandyade, Diet (Herbs in the Diet), Drinks, Nettle* and *Nutrition.*

HICCUPS

See *Dill Water.*

HONEYSUCKLE

For centuries, poets have sung the praises of honeysuckle's beauty and sweet perfume, creating images of sun-filled, lazy summer days. Honeysuckle is an 'old-world' plant that should be included in every herb garden, climbing beautifully up a trellis or just rambling across the back fence.

Culpepper, the great seventeenth century herbalist, regarded honeysuckle as *'a hot martial plant in the sign of Cancer, the leaves being put into gargarisms for sore throats',* and it was one of the plants Dioscorides (famous Greek physician and plant expert of the first century AD) recommended for curing hiccups. Later, in the 1500s, celebrated English herbalist John Gerard listed the virtues of honeysuckle, too: *'the floures steeped in oil and set in the Sun, are good to anoint the body that is benummed, and growne very cold'.* And it was one of those flowers listed by Francis Bacon in the seventeenth century in his essay *Of Gardens* whose *'breath'* is *'far sweeter in the air than in the hand'.*

HONEYSUCKLE SYRUP

This is a good syrup to relieve a sore throat. Sip 15 ml whenever required.

> *2½ cups of fresh honeysuckle flowers*
> *1¼ cups of boiling water*
> *half a cup of sugar*

Lightly crush and bruise the honeysuckle petals before pouring boiling water over them. Set them aside to cool, then strain the liquid through muslin into an enamel or stainless steel saucepan, making sure to squeeze and keep all liquid from the petals. Add the sugar and bring slowly to the boil, then simmer gently until the

mixture is of a syrupy consistency. Cool slightly, then pour into a sterilised bottle and seal.

Honeysuckle Ointment

This delightfully fragrant but gentle ointment can be used to soothe minor burns and sunburn.

3 heaped tablespoons of fresh honeysuckle petals
half a cup of petroleum jelly

Crush and bruise the honeysuckle flowers. Put them, and the petroleum jelly, in a small ceramic bowl in a pan of boiling water. Simmer for 20 minutes, stirring occasionally, then strain into a warm sterilised glass jar and leave to cool. Seal and label.

HORSETAIL

Horsetail stems were the natural forerunner to steel wool and synthetic scourers. A plant growing since prehistoric times, horsetail *(Equisetum arvense)* has survived millions of years almost unchanged. It does not flower, but has clusters of frond-like branches on erect stems, the appearance of which has given them their common name of horsetail.

This plant has the amazing ability to absorb very large amounts of silica, giving it the texture of fine sandpaper. Because of this quality, it has been used both medicinally and as a natural metal cleaner and polish.

Horsetail can be easily grown in the home garden and will grow anywhere except in very alkaline soils. It is a perennial that loves moisture and develops from spores, and is available from most herb nurseries.

Long before steel was even thought of, people were using this plant to clean the dirtiest pots and pans, to clean and polish pewter, brass and copper, and to scour wooden containers and milk pails.

To clean pots, simply rub a handful of dried, leafless horsetail stems onto the surface, then rinse with water to remove any residual green stains.

Medicinally, a decoction was used to stop external or internal bleeding and it was also used as a diuretic. Today, its rich silica

content makes it an excellent ingredient for lotions to improve the strength of nails and add lustre to dull hair.

METAL CLEANER AND POLISH

250 g of fresh horsetail
1.25 litres of cold water
methylated spirits, sufficient

Place the herb in an enamel or stainless steel pan, add the water and allow to infuse overnight. Boil for 15 minutes, remove from heat, allow to cool, and strain through muslin, keeping the herbal liquid. Add 5 ml (1 teaspoon) of methylated spirits to every 300 to 500 ml of liquid or part thereof.

Rub the metal pieces with a cloth soaked in the solution and leave to dry. Polish off with a soft cloth.

NAIL STRENGTHENER

Brittle fingernails can be strengthened by soaking them in a horsetail solution for 15 minutes morning and night.

50 g of dried horsetail
1½ tablespoons of dried dill seed
900 ml water

Put the dried herbs in an enamel or stainless steel saucepan, add the water, bring to the boil and then reduce to a simmer for 20 minutes. Remove from heat, cover, steep for three hours, then strain through muslin cloth, keeping the herbal liquid. Store in a tightly sealed bottle in the refrigerator and use within seven days. Discard immediately if the solution begins to smell rancid, and make a new batch.

HYGIENE

If we shower daily and wear clean clothes, applying expensive toiletries designed to mask body odours is usually unnecessary. However, sometimes Nature does need a little help, and something as simple and inexpensive as a herbal deodorant, which will control unpleasant odour without inhibiting perspiration, is all that's needed.

A light dusting of bicarbonate of soda under the arms is simple, safe and effective. Or a solution of bicarbonate of soda and water can be poured into a refillable roll-on bottle and used like a purchased roll-on deodorant.

An effective herbal deodorant can be made with herbs and cider vinegar. It will have both a subdued perfume and antiseptic properties, and will keep you feeling fresh and odour free. Herbs suitable to use in a liquid deodorant are rosemary, thyme, lavender, sage, lovage, eau-de-cologne mint, spearmint, scented geranium (*Pelargonium*) leaves, eucalyptus, marjoram and honeysuckle flowers. The scented geraniums, which are easy to propagate and grow in most climates, provide a varying range of fragrances and are ideally suited as deodorant herbs.

Other common natural deodorant fragrances include nutmeg, rose, coconut, lime, apple and peppermint.

Natural Deodorant

To make your herbal deodorant, place 3 tablespoons of dried herb or 6 tablespoons of dried flower petals in a ceramic bowl. If it's more convenient to use fresh herbs and flowers, double the quantity. Mix together 300 ml each of apple cider vinegar and distilled water and, in an enamel or stainless steel saucepan, heat to just below boiling point. Pour the liquid over the herbs, cover tightly with plastic wrap and leave to steep for 12 hours. Strain and dilute 50/50 with distilled water if you find the fragrance too strong. Store in a bottle with a tight-fitting lid and, after washing and drying under the arms, dab on the natural deodorant and allow to dry.

After-bath Powder

If you like to use a powder after a bath or shower, you'll find this herbal powder an aromatic delight. Its mild deodorant properties and elusive scent will keep you feeling fresh.

Mix together 75 grams each of rice flour and cornflour and 1 tablespoon of orris root powder (available from herb specialty shops or dried potpourri herb suppliers). Add 1 teaspoon of an essential oil of your choice and 3 teaspoons of distilled water. Mix the oil and water thoroughly through the powder until it feels dry.

Extra oil can be added if the scent is not strong enough, but take care not to get the mixture too wet. If it does become a little too wet, adjust by adding more powder, a little at a time. Once dry, sieve twice and store in a plastic bottle with holes pierced through its lid for shaking out the powder.

INDIGESTION

It's important to remember not to eat while your stomach is upset. You can eat light foods once treatment with a remedy has commenced, but only when you feel some form of appetite. Don't eat for the sake of eating. Acceptable types of food are porridge, light vegetable soup, salads, a small amount of toasted wholemeal bread, grated apple and rice.

Dissolve half a teaspoon of bicarbonate of soda in a glass of hot water and sip this to help fight off an attack of indigestion.

Peppermint and rosemary tea is also helpful in easing indigestion. Steep 1 teaspoon of dried peppermint and 1 teaspoon of dried rosemary in a cup of boiling water, strain into another cup, reheat if required, add a slice of lemon and sweeten with honey. Drink 1 cup morning and night.

A cup of peppermint tea first thing every morning is a good preventative.

Raw cabbage and raw potato will help to relieve this problem. Liquidise half a cabbage and potato in a blender, then press through a fine wire sieve. Dilute a cupful of the juice with half a cup of cooled boiled water and sip slowly throughout the day.

Include herbs and spices such as coriander, fennel and aniseed in your cooking to help prevent indigestion. A glassful of fresh carrot juice each morning on rising will also help to regulate the digestive process. And to prevent embarrassing wind, include oranges in your daily diet.

Persistent indigestion should be investigated by your health practitioner.

See also Digestion and Dill Water.

INK

Scented ink gives a delicate fragrance to personal letters that will waft out as soon as the envelope is opened.

You can make your own ink from plants such as inkbush (*Phytolacca octandra*), mulberries or black (not deadly) nightshade (*Solanum nigrum*) berries and scented with fragrant herbs.

Use herbs that have a strong fragrance, such as lavender, rosemary, rose petals, lemon verbena or hyssop. Dried herbs give the best effect.

Essential oils can also be used for aromatic inks, and are a quick and easy choice if you don't have the time to make ink from scratch. Just add 2 drops of a chosen essential oil to every 1 ml of a bottle of store-bought ink. Remember, ink has its own scent, so choose oils with a strong fragrance.

BASIC INK

Crush the fruit of the inkbush, mulberries or nightshade and squeeze out all the juice. Wear rubber gloves to avoid staining your hands and an apron to protect your clothing.

Gently warm the juice and add 1 teaspoon of arrowroot to every 80 ml of the juice to thicken it. Stir continuously until the mixture thickens and loses its cloudy appearance. Store this basic ink in a small, sealed glass bottle or jar.

LAVENDER INK

15 g of dried lavender flowers
120 ml of water
125 ml of basic ink

Crush the lavender and put it into a saucepan with the water. Bring to the boil and simmer for about 30 minutes or until you are left with 40 ml of liquid. Strain through muslin cloth, squeezing all liquid from the herbs. Blend this herbal liquid with the basic ink.

If the ink is not thick enough, adjust by gently warming and adding a little more arrowroot.

LEMON VERBENA INK

25 g of dried lemon verbena
125 ml of water
125 ml of basic ink

Prepare as for lavender ink.

HYSSOP INK

25 g of dried hyssop
125 ml of water
125 ml of basic ink

Prepare as for lemon verbena ink.

Alternative Method for Fragrant Ink

25 g of dried fragrant herb
100 ml of water
125 ml of basic ink

Prepare as for lavender, lemon verbena and hyssop ink, but reduce the herbal water to 20 ml for a much stronger fragrance.

See also Paper (Scented Writing Paper).

INSECT PESTS

During summer, we are besieged with numerous insect pests that not only annoy and irritate us, but often spoil outdoor activities. Flies and mosquitoes, especially, are a nuisance at this time of the year.

Herbs and essential oils are by far a better way of dealing with these pests than harmful, chemical-based concoctions. Flies particularly dislike lavender oil, while peppermint oil will keep mosquitoes away.

Many herbs can also help to deter these insects, such as lavender, sweet woodruff, lemon verbena, star anise, tansy, any of the mints, thyme, rosemary, bay, camomile, rue, elder, mugwort, southernwood and basil. Combine any of these — the more the better — and tie them in muslin or hessian bags. Hang these bags around the house to deter flies and other insects.

Mosquitoes will stay clear of plants such as cedronella — a herbaceous bush with ferny lemon-scented leaves and pink to violet coloured flowers — and citronella-scented geraniums (pelargoniums). Plant cedronella bushes throughout the garden, close to doorways and outdoor entertainment areas. They will thrive in large pots, which can be placed along verandahs or in other strategic spots.

A personal repellent will help to make outdoor activities pest free and more enjoyable, and is quite easily made from a blend of essential oils. Thoroughly mix together 4 drops each of thyme, lavender and peppermint oil with 8 drops of lemongrass oil and blend with 95 ml of almond oil and 5 ml of wheatgerm oil. Store in an airtight, amber-coloured bottle and use as required, applying liberally to the skin. This all-purpose repellent will discourage flies, mosquitoes, midges and sandflies from attacking you.

See also Creepy-crawlies, Fly Repellents, Garden Sense, Garden Spray, and the individual entries for insects.

IRON

Iron is vital to the growth of any living organism. It not only burns up a lot of impurities, it has regenerative properties as well, transporting oxygen to every cell in the body.

Women are more likely to be deficient in iron than men because they lose about 15 to 30 mg of iron every menstrual period. If this loss is not overcome by including high natural sources of iron in the diet, anaemia can result.

Red meat is the richest source of this mineral in the animal protein group, followed by chicken and fish. However iron can also be obtained from other sources — an important factor for vegetarians and those with high cholesterol problems to consider. There is an abundance of it in all green, leafy vegetables, particularly in the darker leaves. Iron is also present in high concentrations in some seeds, particularly in the germ of wheat. A generous spoonful of wheatgerm sprinkled over your breakfast cereal will almost be enough for your daily requirement.

Natural unprocessed bran gives you plenty of iron and tones up your bowels as well. Fresh and dried pumpkin seeds are high in this mineral, and sesame seeds follow not far behind. Herbal teas, such as those mae with alfalfa and yellow dock, will add to your iron intake, and soya beans are exceedingly iron rich, as are most of the bean family.

Oatmeal is good iron food and will give you a good start to the day; you can get your daily ration from your porridge, if that's what you prefer. Add fresh seasonal fruit and some wheatgerm and you have a super get-up-and-go breakfast.

Egg yolks are acceptable, as they provie iron of animal origin that's easily assimilated.

Yoghurt also contains this mineral. It is an excellent food to include in your diet if your digestion is weak, or if you are recovering from an illness.

All leafy green vegetables, with the exception of spinach (oxalic acid, found in spinach, inhibits the body from using the iron present), are a good source of this mineral.

Dandelion leaf, a common wild herb found growing almost everywhere, is rich in iron and also includes every other vital mineral needed by the body. Young leaves can be added to summer salads along with other greens, or cooked in the same way as spinach.

IRRITABILITY

See Fatigue.

ITCHINESS

See Tea Tree Oil.

JASMINE FURNITURE POLISH

This natural beeswax polish will add a gentle floral fragrance to furniture, as well as making it shine. It will also fill the room the table stands in with a beautiful aroma.

200 g grated beeswax
200 ml mineral turpentine
jasmine essential oil

Grate beeswax into a wide-mouthed, screw-top jar, cover with turpentine, replace lid and leave to stand for at least two weeks, shaking the jar occasionally and adding a little more turpentine as necessary to create the consistency of a smooth paste.

After allowing to stand up to two weeks, stir in jasmine oil one drop at a time until sufficiently scented.

See also Cleaners (Timber Furniture Cleaner and Polish), Lemon Timber Polish, Polish and Polishing Cloth.

JOJOBA CLEANSING OIL

Excellent for cleansing facial skin and removing make-up.

75 ml jojoba oil
10 ml avocado oil
25 ml apricot oil
15 drops essential oil of rose

Add the oils to an amber-coloured glass bottle with a tight-fitting lid. Shake vigorously to blend and store in the refrigerator.

To use, pour sufficient oil onto a piece of cotton wool and gently apply to face and neck until clean, wiping in outward and upward movements. Remove oily residue with an alcohol-free toning lotion, such as witch hazel (available from pharmacies), then moisturise.

See also Herbal Skin Care and Skin.

JOJOBA MOISTURISING LOTION

100 ml glycerin
5 ml avocado oil
75 ml rose-water
8 drops lemon juice
60 ml jojoba oil
12 drops essential oil of rose
5 ml wheatgerm oil

Add all the ingredients to an amber-coloured glass bottle. Seal tightly and shake vigorously until all the ingredients have been completely emulsified.

Apply as required, rubbing well into the skin.

See also Herbal Skin Care and Skin.

KIDS

Home-made herbal products for use at bath-time are a great way to introduce children to herbs and herbal oils for natural body care. It can give them a basic understanding of how and why we should work in harmony with nature and not against it. It's important that our young ones realise from an early age that natural things are the best, the purest and the most beneficial.

BUBBLE BATH

See separate entry under 'B'.

WASH BAGS

Soapy wash bags are great for scrubbing the kids clean and softening their skin at the same time. Simply make a 25-square cm bag from a piece of muslin with a drawstring to close it. Mix together 2 tablespoons of dried herbs — camomile or lavender are excellent — with 2 tablespoons of medium-ground oatmeal and 1 tablespoon of pure, unscented, grated white soap. Place the mixture in the bag, and show the kids how to use their wash bags in the bath.

HAIR CONDITIONER

Put the lustre back into your child's hair if it is dry and lifeless by saturating his or her locks with a vitalising combination of equal quantities of olive, almond and avocado oils gently warmed to room temperature. Wrap his or her head in a thick, warm towel and leave for 15 minutes before rinsing off. Repeat weekly until no longer necessary.

HEAD LICE

Combine 25 drops each of rosemary and lavender oil, 13 drops of geranium oil and 12 drops of eucalyptus oil in an egg cup with 75 ml of almond oil, and blend well. Using a comb, divide the hair of the affected child into small sections and saturate each section down to the roots with the mixture. Pile long hair on top of the head, making sure that every strand is oiled.

Wrap plastic around the child's head and behind the ears to stop the oils from evaporating. Make sure small children can't move the plastic anywhere near their nose or mouth and by doing so restrict their breathing.

Leave on for two hours, then remove the plastic. Apply water to the hair, and shampoo well. Rinse thoroughly and comb through with a fine comb. Repeat three days later.

KITTY LITTER

Commercial kitty litter is no more than diatomaceous earth, made from the finely ground skeletons of marine creatures called diatoms. It has great absorbent qualities — and is excellent for cleaning oil and grease from concrete driveways.

Dampen the concrete, spread the litter, leave on overnight then brush with a very stiff yard broom.

See also Grease (Driveways).

LAURDRY SENSE

Most laundry cupboards are cluttered with a wide array of products that promise to bleach, whiten, soften and clean. They also cause the highest levels of domestic pollution.

As responsible members of the community, it is up to every one of us to ensure our water is as biodegradable (capable of being decomposed by bacteria or other natural means) as possible.

You'll be able to use the following laundry solutions with confidence and a clear conscience.

FABRIC SOFTENER

Soak garments overnight in a solution of 1 part vinegar to 3 parts water, then rinse well in clear water before washing. Alternatively, use less soap in your washing machine and make up the difference with bicarbonate of soda — 1 part bicarbonate of soda to 3 parts soap powder will leave your clothes feeling soft.

Hard water can be softened with the addition of a handful of washing soda (available from supermarkets) to the wash and rinse cycles.

These laundry solutions are environmentally friendly, safe, inexpensive and will do just as good a job as the expensive chemical softeners.

FINAL RINSE TIPS

Add half a cup of white vinegar to the final rinse cycle to remove all traces of soap or detergent, or 1 cup of white vinegar to eliminate fluff or lint on your sheets.

LAUNDRY TUB CARE

Keep stainless-steel tubs and taps clean by scouring with bicarbonate of soda or non-iodised salt. Rinse off then give a final wipe over with a weak solution of vinegar and water to produce a sparkling surface free of streaks.

MAKE YOUR OWN STARCH

If you still use starch, a strong, natural starch can be made from old potatoes. Grate them coarsely under water, leave the mash to soak for 24 hours, strain off the dirty liquid, and spread the potatoes on trays to dry. You will be left with a powdered starch which you should store in an airtight container.

WHITEN YOUR OWN CLOTHES

Add half a cup of borax to the normal wash cycle then hang the clothes in the sun to dry for brightness to rival that given by any commercial product.

WASHING MACHINE CARE

Add 3 cups of white vinegar to a normal warm-water cycle with no clothes in the machine to give both the machine and the hoses a good clean.

Repeat the procedure about every three months and you'll save on costly repair bills.

WASHING WOOLLEN GARMENTS

Woollen garments will retain their natural softness if washed in a solution of 1 tablespoon of borax to every 5 litres of warm soapy water. Rinse well.

To preserve the natural softness of woollen blankets, add 1 tablespoon of glycerin (for each blanket) to warm soapy water. Wash on a gentle cycle, rinse well (adding a drop or two of lavender oil to the final rinse), spin, then air dry.

For protection against moths during storage, add a few drops of eucalyptus or lavender oil to a face washer and include in the final rinse.

See also Bacteria Busters, Clothes, Eucalyptus Oil and Lavender (Lavender Wool Wash).

LAVENDER

And Lavender, Whose spikes of azure bloom
Shall be erewhile in arid bundles bound,
To lurk amidst her labours of the loom,
And crown her kerchiefs with mickle rare perfume...

Shenstone

One of the best known and loved of all the herbs, the many varieties of lavender are grown in gardens everywhere, even when no special thought has been given to herbs as such.

Lavender's use for cosmetic and aromatic purposes can be traced back to the Greeks and Romans. This highly aromatic herb was probably introduced to Britain during Roman occupation, and its use eventually spread with British colonisation.

The English, French and Italian varieties of lavender are the more commonly known.

ENGLISH LAVENDER

The dried flowers of English lavender (*Lavandula spicata*) are used in potpourri and herb sachets, and the essential oil may be included in natural cosmetics, bath preparations and soap.

It prefers full sun in temperate climates, but might need protection in warmer climates. This species has lovely true lilac flowers on graceful stems.

FRENCH LAVENDER

This is a perennial shrub which grows to around a metre high and wide, and produces short, soft-stemmed, plump spikes of dark lavender flowers in warmer months. French lavender (*Lavandula dentata*) is suitable for warmer climates and humid coastal areas.

This lavender's scent has just a hint of camphor. It does not have long-lasting qualities when dried.

ITALIAN LAVENDER

A hardy, dense and compact shrub that is a prolific flowerer in both spring and autumn, Italian lavender (*Lavandula stoechas*) produces spikes of dark purple flowers and is suitable for warm and humid coastal areas. Its uses are similar to those of English lavender, and it has a hint of camphor and minty undertones.

LAVENDER BATH WATER

Add this fragrant water to your bath to relieve sore muscles and prevent skin dryness.

Put 2 generous handfuls of dried lavender buds in a ceramic bowl. Mix together 500 ml each of distilled water and cider vinegar in a non-metallic saucepan and bring to just below boiling point. Pour the liquid over the herbs, seal the bowl with plastic wrap and allow to steep for 12 hours. Strain mixture through fine muslin, squeezing and keeping all liquid from the herbs. Bottle for future use.

Add 1 cup of lavender water to your bath while the water is running from the taps.

LAVENDER HONEY

Serve this delicious herbal treat on freshly baked crusty bread or, during winter when colds and flu are prevalent, add a spoonful to a hot lemon drink and let its antiseptic qualities ease a sore throat.

Gently warm a bottle of light honey in a double boiler, add 1 to 2 tablespoons of dried lavender flowers (English lavender is best), and allow to infuse for two minutes. Remove from heat and allow to stand in the hot sun for a few hours — a sunny windowsill away from ants and other creatures is ideal. Strain out the lavender flowers and bottle.

LAVENDER TEA

A tea made from the heads of lavender flowers is an ideal remedy for people with a sensitive, gentle nature who suffer from nervousness, headaches, migraine, dizziness and fainting spells.

To prepare lavender tea, add 1 level teaspoon of dried flower heads to a ceramic cup, pour in hot water, cover, infuse for three minutes, and strain into another cup. Reheat if necessary.

If brewing in a teapot, allow 1 teaspoon per person and one for the pot. Pour on boiling water, infuse for five minutes then strain into individual cups. Use only a ceramic teapot set aside specifically for brewing herbal teas.

LAVENDER WOOL WASH

This is excellent for washing your blankets and woollens, and will leave them with just a hint of lavender fragrance.

4 teaspoons dried lavender
1 litre boiling water
500 g grated, pure soap
1 tablespoon borax

Put the dried herbs in a ceramic bowl and pour in the boiling water. Cover, steep overnight, then strain through muslin cloth and keep the lavender water.

Combine the grated soap, lavender water and borax in a saucepan. Bring to the boil, stirring constantly until well blended. Remove from heat and cool. You will have a soft, white, jelly-like substance. Store in a wide-mouthed jar and seal securely.

Wash woollens by hand, using ½ to 1 cup of the mixture, or 2 to 3 cups in the washing machine for blankets; rinse well in clean water.

See also Cleaners (Lavender Cleanser).

LEATHER LOUNGES

See Lounges (Leather).

LEGS

Legs, and in particular the thighs, need continual attention to avoid cellulite developing or to help alleviate this problem. Swimming, dancing, cycling and yoga exercises are all ideal for keeping the leg muscles toned.

Friction massage with a loofah during a warm bath is good for accelerating cell metabolism and improving the circulation. Coarse sea salt (available from health-food stores) applied to the loofah during massage helps to improve skin colour, and is excellent for clearing flaking skin and surface spots. Always massage upwards in the direction of the heart.

Lower legs also suffer from the same problems. As with thighs, exfoliating with a loofah should be done regularly each week at bath-time. Deal with more stubborn areas with coarse sea salt or a bath bag filled with oatmeal and camomile mixture. Rinse off thoroughly, then massage with a good moisturising cream, like the one following.

Melt together in a double stainless-steel or enamel pan, over a low heat, 50 grams anhydrous lanolin (wool fat, available from pharmacies), 50 ml of olive oil and 25 ml of either almond oil or apricot kernel oil. When completely liquid, pour into a suitable, sterilised, screw-top jar and allow to cool.

Massage into feet, legs and knees, and arms and elbows, smoothing it firmly upwards.

LEMON JUICE

STAINED CUTLERY
For stubborn stains, dissolve a little salt in lemon juice and rub over cutlery with a soft cloth. Rinse the cutlery in warm water and rub with a chamois.

HANDS
To remove unpleasant or strong odours from hands work half a lemon into the skin.

For dish-pan hands mix equal parts of lemon juice and glycerin and keep next to the sink. Apply to damp hands whenever needed, massaging well into the skin.

OLD-FASHIONED HAND LOTION
This lotion will not only clean and nourish the hands, but will also strengthen the nails.

> *50 ml lemon juice*
> *50 ml rose-water*
> *50 ml glycerin*

Put all the ingredients in a glass bottle, seal, and shake vigorously to mix.

MILDEW

Remove mildew on garments by sponging with lemon juice and then placing the garment in the sun until the spores have gone (usually one day).

PERSPIRATION STAINS

Perspiration marks on woollen garments can be removed by sponging with lemon juice and water. Hang garments to air after cleaning.

SAUCEPANS

When boiling eggs, add a small slice of lemon to the water to prevent saucepans from discolouring.

LEMON TIMBER POLISH

To make an environmentally friendly liquid furniture polish that will keep all timber surfaces shiny and clean simply dissolve 1 teaspoon of lemon oil or 2 ml of your favourite essential oil, in 600 ml of olive oil. Apply with a clean, soft cloth.

See also Cleaners (Timber Furniture Cleaner and Polish), Jasmine Furniture Polish, Polish and Polishing Cloth.

LICE

See Kids.

LIP GLOSS

See Herbal Make-up.

LIPSTICK

See Herbal Make-up.

LOUNGES

FABRIC

By virtue of continuous human use, fabric-covered lounge suites tend to become grease-stained, and need regular care and cleaning. Use the following natural fabric cleaner.

Thoroughly mix together equal amounts of borax powder, salt and powdered kaolin (available from pharmacies) to make a base. Rub dried lavender buds through a fine wire sieve to reduce to a powder and mix 1 teaspoon of the powdered herb to every cup of the base mixture. Once made, store in an airtight jar in a dry, cool, dark place for 24 hours before use to allow absorption of the subtle lavender fragrance.

Sprinkle this powder all over the fabric, paying particular attention to the arms and headrests. Spread it evenly over the soiled areas with the palms of your hands and leave overnight or for at least 12 hours, then rub the fabric with a clean, coarse towel and vacuum the powder off.

LEATHER

Most leather lounges will come clean with no more than warm soapy water. However, if your lounge has become grubby from an accumulation of different stains it should be treated with talcum powder first.

Sprinkle the powder over the stained areas, rub in thoroughly with the palm of your hand, then roughly rub with a towel. Next, dissolve some pure soap flakes in warm water and rub all over the furniture, paying careful attention to the soiled areas, with a towel wrung out in this soapy water.

Allow 24 hours after cleaning is complete for the leather to dry and become firm, then finish off with the following wax polishing paste and buff with a dry, soft cloth.

Stains on leather lounges can also be removed by rubbing with eucalyptus

oil, using a circular motion. Test a small section first in a spot that is not noticeable.

LEMON POLISHING PASTE

30 g grated beeswax
1½ tablespoons natural turpentine
6 drops lemon oil

Melt the beeswax in a double saucepan over a medium heat. When completely liquid, turn heat to low and add the turpentine, stirring until well blended. Remove from heat, stir in lemon oil and store in a sealed wide-mouthed glass jar.

MAKE-UP

See Herbal Make-up.

MEN

Very seldom are men considered when it comes to natural skin care and home-made herbal products. Yet we all know the adverse effect continual shaving can have upon facial skin, and worse still the drying effect of an alcohol-based after shave lotion. It can all add up to an irritating skin rash, or even more serious conditions like eczema.

Bit by bit, men who were once cool as cucumbers are warming to the concept of natural skin care. Today's man is now realising the benefits of natural, herbal based products.

ROSE-WATER LOTION

To keep facial skin supple and in good condition, a moisturising lotion should be applied to facial skin and the neck immediately after shaving and toning.

A suitable moisturising lotion can be made by blending together 180 ml of rose-water, 40 ml of almond oil, 20 ml of glycerine and 10 ml of witch hazel. Beat all the ingredients until the mixture emulsifies. Store in a suitable bottle and shake well before using.

Apply to face and neck and gently massage in with your fingertips. Massaging the skin is also good for the circulation.

BEARDS AND MOUSTACHES

Beards and moustaches also require attention and regular grooming. Wash them every time you wash your face, using your fingertips to massage the skin underneath. Dry, then apply a herbal oil such as basil, rosemary or sage.

To apply the oil, rub a little of it between the palms of the hand and stroke a good quality hairbrush over them to pick up the oil. Run the hairbrush through the beard and moustache — if this is too difficult, use a toothbrush.

MICE

See Rats.

MIDGES

Dilute 3 drops of thyme oil in 5 ml of lemon juice and apply to the bites. This will stop the irritation.

MILDEW

See Mould & Mildew; Lemon Juice.

MINERALS

Minerals control the body's chemical balance and an adequate intake is necessary if you are to achieve the ideal state of physical equilibrium. The mineral requirements of your body differ from time to time and it is therefore important to maintain a balanced intake of correct foodstuffs to keep your body functioning in peak condition.

CALCIUM

Calcium ensures healthy bones and teeth and proper processing of all vitamins in the food we consume. It stimulates enzyme activity and is important for a healthy heart.

CHLORINE

Chlorine combines with natural sodium to act as a body cleanser.

IODINE

Iodine is a vital element in the health and correct activity of the thyroid gland. This gland directly or indirectly controls every metabolic process, so good function must be maintained.

IRON

Vital to healthy growth and healthy living, iron is essential for our blood to be able to carry oxygen throughout the body.

See also separate listing, Iron.

MAGNESIUM

Essential for the good health of the central nervous system, and indeed the whole of your body, magnesium is the mineral that helps you walk around feeling fully alive. It also plays an important role in hardening teeth and preventing tooth decay.

PHOSPHORUS

Phosphorus helps the nervous system remain healthy and at peak performance. It has a tonic effect on the circulation and is essential for maintaining healthy skin, hair and fingernails.

POTASSIUM

Along with sodium, potassium helps to help regulate the balance of body fluid. Natural sources of potassium and sodium are: celery, cucumber, lettuce, cabbage, cauliflower, tomato, watercress and dandelion greens.

SILICON

Silicon is important for healthy fingernails and hair, and helps prevent calcium deposits around joints.

SODIUM

Sufficient free natural sodium in the diet can preserve suppleness and ease of movement and also aid in keeping the degenerative processes of old age at bay. However, it must be remembered that consumption of natural sodium does not mean the use of commercially available salt, or of salt found in heavily processed foods — it means the intake of the mineral in sufficient quantities as it occurs naturally in food.

SULPHUR

Sulphur has a cleansing and antiseptic action on the whole of the digestive tract. It is needed for the formation of amino acids, the

metabolism of proteins, and can be helpful with skin irritation conditions, especially those that do not respond to silicon.

TRACE MINERALS

Most of the trace minerals seem to appear in the glandular system, and the part they play in good health is not yet fully understood.

See also Diet (Herbs in the Diet), Nutrition and Vitamins.

MOSQUITO BITE

Apply undiluted lavender oil to the bite. If you have been bitten over a large area, dilute 10 drops of lavender oil and 5 drops of thyme oil in 250 ml of cider vinegar, and add this mixture to a warm bath. After bathing, apply undiluted lavender oil to all the bites.

See also Stings and Bites.

MOSQUITO CONTROL

At the very least, mosquitoes are annoying and can make outdoor entertainment and activities quite unpleasant. Controlling these pests is not about mass murdering them, but about deterring them from annoying us or entering our living space.

Fortunately there are safe, natural ways in which we can do this without having to resort to chemicals that pollute the air we breathe and that can endanger the health of our family.

It goes without saying that one of the best control methods around the home is properly installed insect screens and doors. Those mosquitoes that do still manage to find their way in can be safely dispatched with the following herbal spray:

MOSQUITO SPRAY

A home-made garlic mosquito spray is an effective control method and doesn't smell as strongly as you might expect, nor linger when sprayed.

Add 100 grams of unpeeled garlic cloves and 50 ml of

mineral oil (or vegetable oil) to a glass jar. Seal tightly and leave to steep for 24 hours. Strain, dilute 5 parts of the garlic mixture with 1 part of water and add 5 ml of methylated spirits to every 500 ml of liquid. Store in a glass bottle with a non-metallic lid.

This spray is not poisonous to humans or pets, and will kill mosquitoes and their larvae if sprayed around a room.

MOSQUITO REPELLENT

See Eucalyptus oil.

MOULD AND MILDEW

Bathrooms, laundries, kitchens, cupboards, wardrobes, dresser drawers and book shelves are the most likely places for mould and mildew to grow. Also, a greasy film on kitchen walls and poorly ventilated bathrooms will create the perfect atmosphere for these unsightly looking spores.

Natural solutions are very effective in controlling this problem. However, they should be performed in conjunction with other preventive measures.

* Try to control areas of dampness around the house. Ensure that under-house areas and basement rooms are adequately ventilated. Replace cracked and defective mortar and make sure that outside drainage is adequate.
* In crawl spaces under the house, spread a layer of moisture barrier material over the soil — consult your local hardware store or builders' supplier.
* Clear away overhanging trees, creepers and shrubs from around the home. Check for leaking pipes or taps.
* Check hidden areas such as the tops of blinds, pelmets, high windowsills and doorjambs for dust. These areas make an ideal growing area, as dust and mould tend to live together.

When you have given your home the once-over, you can then try the following solutions (overleaf) to solve any mould and mildew problem you may have.

DAMPNESS

You can get rid of dampness in the house by heating for a short time, then opening doors and windows to let out the moisture-laden air. In bathrooms, kitchens and laundries, install effective ventilation exhaust fans.

WARDROBES

To dry the air in wardrobes and other small storage areas, burn an electric light continuously until all signs of dampness have gone. The heat generated will be sufficient provided the area is not too large. Keep clothing and other items away from the bulb to prevent the possibility of a fire hazard. Install some form of permanent ventilation to prevent the problem recurring.

WALLS, CEILINGS AND TILES

Mould can usually be removed from walls, tiles and ceilings with bicarbonate of soda, vinegar and hot water. Mix a quantity of bicarbonate of soda in hot water and apply this solution to the affected areas with a clean cloth. Rinse off with another clean cloth and hot water, then apply a solution of vinegar and hot water with a third cloth. Rinse off with a fourth cloth and hot water, remembering to keep the rinsing cloths in separate buckets.

BOOKS

Remove mildew from books with a soft cloth dipped in vinegar or lemon juice. Wipe over with a clean cloth straight away. To prevent the problem recurring, don't pack or compress books tightly together on shelves. Leave enough room for air to circulate. Sprinkle a few drops of oil of cloves or eucalyptus oil over bookcase shelves to prevent mildew from forming on the books.

PICNIC UMBRELLAS

When your favourite picnic umbrella comes out of storage, use a hand brush to remove any mildew spores. (Do this out-of-doors, otherwise you'll have mould spores flying in all directions, eager to start up new areas of mildew.) Wash with hot water and soap, then sun dry. If any mildew areas remain treat them with half a lemon dipped in salt, rubbing until all traces have disappeared.

WOOLLEN BLANKETS

Mouldy areas on woollen blankets can be covered with a paste made from salt and lemon juice. Leave on overnight then brush the paste off and wash the blanket in the usual way. Hang it in full sun for a day.

BLINDS

Bonded blinds can be wash over with soap, then wiped with a damp cloth.

Bamboo blinds should be washed with a solution of ¼ cup of salt, 1 tablespoon of bicarbonate of soda and 1 litre of water. Rinse clean, dry, and rub lightly with raw linseed oil. To remove mildew stains from venetian blinds, mix together some fine emery powder and linseed oil. Rub well onto the affected area.

CURTAINS

First brush mildew spores off with a hard brush, rub with a cut lemon dipped in salt, then wash. If curtains are too heavy for your machine, mouldy areas should first be rubbed with eucalyptus oil, left for a few hours, and then wiped clean with a damp cloth.

Nylon curtains can be soaked in a solution of ½ cup of vinegar and 5 litres of cold water.

REFRIGERATOR DOOR SEALS

Fungus and mould that forms on refrigerator door seals should first be scrubbed well with a toothbrush and toothpaste and then wiped off with clean water. Heavy mould may require several applications. Finally, wipe down with lemon juice on a clean cloth. Natural alternatives often require a little more patience and elbow grease, but their results are just as effective as those obtained from their chemical cousins.

EUCALYPTUS MOULD SPRAY

This solution will remove surface mould from tiles and painted surfaces, and also acts as a natural disinfectant.

Dissolve 20 ml of eucalyptus oil in 20 ml of methylated spirits and add to a pump-spray bottle containing 500 ml of water. Shake well to mix.

Spray over affected area, a small section at a time, and wipe off. For stubborn mould, use a little 'elbow grease'.

MUSCULAR ACHES AND PAINS

Soak in a hot bath in which ½ cup of bicarbonate of soda has been dissolved. Follow this by massaging the painful and aching areas with the following ointment: crush 2 garlic cloves and mix well with 100 grams of Vaseline. Store in a jar with an airtight lid.

See also Tea Tree Oil and Witch Hazel Ointment.

NAILS

See Horsetail.

NAPPY RASH

Garlic water or oil applied externally will help to soothe irritation. To make garlic oil, chop up 6 garlic cloves and add to 500 ml of sunflower oil in a glass jar. Seal tightly, stand for ten days, strain and store in an airtight glass bottle.

Alternatively, you can bathe the affected area with Camomile Nappy Wash whenever the nappy is changed.

CAMOMILE NAPPY WASH

1 cup dried camomile flowers
1 cup dried elder flowers
boiling water

Put the herbs in a ceramic bowl, add sufficient boiling water to cover by about 2 cm, cover the bowl and allow to infuse overnight. Next day, strain through clean muslin cloth, squeezing all liquid from the herbs, and store the liquid in a sterilised, airtight bottle in the refrigerator for no longer than seven days. If the lotion begins to smell unpleasant any earlier than seven days after making it, discard and make a fresh batch.

NASAL CONGESTION

See Tea Tree Oil.

NAUSEA

Freshly grated ginger or powdered cinnamon infused with hot water, or sprinkled in other herbal teas, can be taken as required to relieve the symptoms of nausea and vomiting.

Clove tea is another excellent remedy for allaying nausea and vomiting, while at the same time stimulating the digestive system. Add 10 cloves to a ceramic cup, pour 250 ml of boiling water over them, cover and infuse for 10 minutes. Reheat if required and take as necessary.

NERVOUS TENSION

The herb valerian is a very powerful natural sedative and tranquilliser and, unlike its synthetic counterpart, is not habit forming. Take it as a cold tea to relieve nervous tension, insomnia and restlessness.

The tea is made by infusing the dried root in boiling water and allowing to stand for twelve hours. The tea is slightly bitter and the taste can be improved by the addition of honey. Drink no more than 3 cups in any one day.

NETTLE

Depending upon your point of view, a stinging nettle is either a very useful plant or an unattractive weed that stings when touched. With care, the nettle can be enjoyed and employed, as the leaves lose their sting when boiled or dried.

Every part of the plant — leaf, root and seed — is rich in vitamins, iron, protein, silicic acid, nitrogen, chlorophyll and other trace elements. The nettle provides a nutritional, staple green that can be enjoyed in summer salads or cooked like spinach.

NETTLE SOUP
1 handful young nettle leaves
400 g potatoes
1 onion, chopped
2 tablespoons butter
2 tablespoons cream
1 litre stock

Wearing rubber gloves, cut nettle stalks and select the youngest and greenest leaves. Cook in a saucepan with half the butter. No extra liquid is needed. Fry the onion and potato in the remaining butter until golden in colour. Add the nettle leaves and stir together. Pour in the stock and cook gently until tender. Add the cream last of all.

NETTLE ALE
A pleasant drink that is also reputed to be good for rheumatism and arthritis.

500 g young nettle leaves
15 g freshly grated ginger
1 large lemon, peeled and juiced
350 g brown sugar
1 slice wholemeal bread
2 teaspoons compressed yeast
1 tablespoon cream of tartar
4 litres water

Place the nettles, ginger and lemon rind in a large pot with the water and bring to the boil. Simmer for 20 minutes and remove from heat. Add sugar and lemon juice and leave to cool. Strain when it reaches room temperature, then add bread, spread with yeast and cream of tartar, and cover. Leave to ferment for two to three days. Remove bread and scum from surface, add a little sugar to taste and bottle. Leave a week before drinking.

See also Drinks (Herbal).

NETTLE HAIR CONDITIONING LOTION

A conditioning lotion that is reputed to prevent falling hair, stimulate growth and leave hair shiny and healthy.

Add a handful of fresh young nettle leaves to an enamel or stainless steel saucepan and cover with almond oil. Bring to just below boiling and simmer until the herbs are crisp. Allow to cool, strain, add a few drops of rosemary oil until it is just fragrant, and store the oil in a tightly sealed bottle.

Massage into the scalp thoroughly two or three times a week after washing your hair.

NICOTINE STAINS

To remove nicotine stains from clothing, sponge with eucalyptus oil, then wash.

NIGHT-TIME PESTS

See Creepy-crawlies and Insect Pests.

NUTRITION

GREAT EATING WITH HERBS

Herbs have always contributed a great deal toward human health. Not only those herbs cultivated in the home garden, but also the wild plants found growing in abundance around the countryside.

The weeds, or wild herbs, that were part of great-grandma's medicine chest are gradually finding their way back into the human diet. Along with their cultivated cousins, they are excellent companions in any salad. They can be juiced for health-giving drinks, taken as a tea or tonic, and included in cooking for extra zest and as a healthy treat. Dried and ground to a fine powder they make a natural spicing for soups and other vegetable dishes.

In most cases, quite a number of wild plants can be found growing in and around your own garden: chickweed, dandelion, lambsquarter, purslane, fat hen, wild mustard, sorrel and shepherd's purse. And if you are unable to identify these plants, your local library can help, as there have been many books published with full colour photographs of the various weeds (wild herbs) found growing in Australia.

The regular use of herbs will add vitamins and minerals to your diet, replace salt as a flavouring agent, help to prevent flatulence and promote better digestion of food, and will transform a good plain meal into a gastronomic delight. Whenever possible, add fresh herbs to your dishes. However, some herbs are not always available fresh throughout the year, in which case dried herbs will suffice.

See also Diet (Herbs in the Diet), Minerals and Vitamins.

Wild Herb Garnish

This makes an excellent salt substitute and can be used wherever you would usually use salt.

Combine 1 tablespoon each of dried, ground fat hen, celery seed, thyme, oregano and toasted sesame seeds, mixing well, and reduce to a powder in a blender, with pestle and mortar, or by rubbing through a fine wire sieve. Store in an airtight jar, label and date, and use within twelve months. If you feel that you still need that salty taste, you can include 2 tablespoons of dried, ground kelp in the mixture.

You will have to gather the fat hen from your garden or in the countryside, but the rest of the ingredients can be obtained from your local health-food store.

It is important to remember that when gathering wild herbs, you must not collect them from the sides of roads or anywhere that they may have been affected by routine chemical spraying.

HERBS IN SALADS

Green salads that include one or two wild herbs or that are generously laced with aromatic herbs have an appealing relish and help to stimulate the appetite, as well as being packed with health-giving properties.

Quantities of fresh parsley and mint, chopped finely, make salads not only delectable but even more nutritious. Borage leaves add a natural, salty flavour, while nasturtium leaves make a useful replacement for pepper.

Herb Salad

This is a delicious salad that is quick and simple to make. It can be eaten on its own as a light and nutritious lunch, or included as a side salad to a main evening meal.

For variety and interest, use two or more different types of lettuce torn into smallish pieces. To this add lots of watercress, alfalfa and red clover sprouts, chives, parsley, and very young

dandelion leaves torn into about 2.5 cm pieces. (Older, larger dandelion leaves have a bitter taste.) Then add smaller amounts of basil, dill, lemon balm and nasturtium leaves, with a very small garnish of mint, oregano and lemon thyme.

Just before serving, you can toss the salad in a wine vinegar. Or better still, one of the many herb vinegars now available.

EATING FOR ENERGY

The notion that you can eat whatever you like as long as you pop a few vitamin pills is a fallacy. It just doesn't work.

Your way of eating largely determines whether you are brimming with energy or dragging yourself through the day and evening. The key to eating for energy is including lots of raw fruits and vegetables in your diet. For maximum vitality, 50–75% of what you eat should be raw.

A diet high in raw foods has been credited with stimulating healing, rejuvenation, an improved mental and emotional state and enhanced athletic performance. Fruit is an ideal food for humankind. It has a great taste, is the easiest food to digest, is the least mucus-inducing, and will open the sinuses to improve breathing.

Because of the citric and other acids found in fruit, it has an acid reaction in the digestion. Yet due to the high content of alkaline-forming minerals in fruit, it has an alkaline reaction in the bloodstream. This helps to neutralise the waste products of metabolism found in the bloodstream, which are always acid. Fruit acts as a natural laxative, promoting the secretory action of the liver, pancreas and other secretory glands.

Whenever possible, eat only organically grown fruit which has been picked when it is almost ready to drop from the tree. It is then at peak ripeness and contains the most juice.

For ease of digestion, you can juice the fruit rather than consume it whole.

Avoid non-organically grown fruit, and also fruit which has been picked unripe or treated with chemicals. Nutritional losses are high when there are long time lapses between the harvesting of the fruit and the time of eating. Try cutting out all highly processed, ready-in-a-minute foods full of chemical additives. Then, along with the fresh fruit, eat a balanced diet of other natural foods, such as fresh vegetables, wholemeal products and pulses or legumes, with smaller quantities of fish, game or free range poultry.

Do this, and your energy levels will begin to soar! Remember, modern processed foods create a congested environment inside your body, which can be a breeding ground for disease.

ODOURS

When homes are kept shut for long periods of time, most notably in winter when we try to prevent cold air from entering and warm air from escaping, odours which usually leave through open windows remain. This can make the air stale and often offensive smelling.

What better way to freshen up a room than with an aromatic air freshener spray? It will not only make your surroundings pleasant, but its natural disinfectant and antiseptic properties will help to control airborne bacteria and viruses.

ANTISEPTIC AIR-FRESHENER SPRAY

To make your fragrant spray, first choose from any of the following essential oils, listed in descending order of their antiseptic powers: thyme, bergamot, juniper, clove, lavender, peppermint, rosemary or eucalyptus. Dissolve 1.5-2 ml of your chosen oil in 5 ml of methylated spirits and then blend this with 500 ml of distilled water. Store in a pump-spray bottle. Shake well to mix and use on a fine mist setting.

OTHER ALTERNATIVES

Sometimes, however, odours may require more specific methods of elimination. The following natural alternatives will help to keep your home fragrantly fresh.

* A few slices of lemon placed in a shallow dish of water will remove the smell of cigarette smoke from a room. If people are continually smoking, or if you need to eliminate the smoke smell of an open fire or fuel stove, put ½ to 1 cup of brown vinegar in the room. This also works well in smelly cupboards, especially those that have a musty or mouldy odour.

* Prevent drawers from becoming musty by placing herb sachets in them. Lavender and other fragrant herbs are ideal. Sachets can be bought in most gift shops, or purchase a bag of loose potpourri and simply add 2 or 3 tablespoons of it to your own home-made small cotton bags.

- To eliminate a musty smell from cupboards, place inside it a cup of boiling water to which has been added a few drops of your favourite essential oil — lavender or rosemary are both excellent for this purpose.
- A cup of rosemary vinegar, or other herbal vinegar, placed close to the stove helps to eliminate cooking odours.
- Deodorise your refrigerator, garbage bin and kitchen compost bin by washing them out with 1 litre of water to which has been added 1 teaspoon of lemon juice.
- Shoe odour can be eliminated by sprinkling powdered herbs, such as dried camomile, in shoes each evening, and making sure that the powder reaches the very tips. Reduce the dried herb to a powder by rubbing through a fine wire sieve.

See also Bacteria Busters, Plastic and Refrigerator.

ONION

The onion is one of the most well known food and medicinal plants in history. It is highly nutritious, an excellent disinfectant, a natural antibiotic, and is rich in vitamin B_1

A regular intake of onion helps the nervous system remain healthy.

Taken as a syrup, it will aid in digestion and will help to relieve the miseries of a cold. A bowl of onion soup will help to bring out a fever and restore lost energy.

ONION SYRUP

1 large grated onion
2 tablespoons honey
1 bottle white wine

Put all the ingredients in a ceramic bowl. Cover and allow to steep for two weeks, making sure to stir the mixture morning and night, every day. Strain through sterile muslin and store the syrup in an airtight glass bottle.

Take 1 tablespoon morning and night when needed.

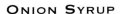

ONION SOUP

2 medium-sized onions
2 medium-sized potatoes
1 litre stock
125 ml light milk
50 g butter
1 garlic clove, crushed
parsley, basil and thyme

Slice the onion and potato. Melt the butter in a pan with a heavy base and add the potato, onion and crushed garlic. Cook over a low heat, stirring from time to time. Mix in the stock, bring to the boil and simmer for about 20 minutes, by which time the vegetables will be tender. Stir in the milk, season with herbs and reheat to simmering point.

Eat as is or process in a blender first.

ORAL HYGIENE

Smile, and the world smiles with you — a well known cliche, but true. If you want a sparkling smile with healthy teeth, it's up to you. That means correct oral hygiene; looking after your gums and teeth is as important as caring for the rest of your body.

Some simple rules to follow, which will help to keep your teeth in top condition, are:

* Brush and floss your teeth at least twice a day.
* Brush your teeth or rinse your mouth after each snack.
* Have a dental check-up twice a year.
* Ensure you eat a well-balanced diet, including herbs that help to keep teeth strong. Healthy teeth need the minerals calcium, magnesium, phosphorus and the trace elements. Herbs to include in the diet are alfalfa, parsley, peppermint, caraway, cayenne, garlic, watercress, chamomile and kelp.

Healthy teeth are not only produced by the use of proprietary brand toothpastes, which quite often promise all sorts of amazing things. Your teeth and gums can be kept in tip-top condition simply by cleaning them with herbs and other natural, safe ingredients.

A quick and simple tooth powder can be made by combining salt and bicarbonate of soda. Thoroughly mix together 2 tablespoons of fine sea salt and 3 tablespoons of bicarbonate of soda and store in a dry, airtight jar. To use, shake a little of the mixture into your hand and pick it up with a damp toothbrush.

Alternatively you can make your own herbal toothpaste which will leave your teeth and gums feeling clean and fresh: dilute 2 drops of peppermint oil in 10 ml of safflower oil, and add to this 2 tablespoons of powdered orris root and 1 tablespoon of quince gel, then mix to the consistency of putty. Store this toothpaste in a sterilised glass jar with a tightly fitting lid. (You can make the gel by bringing to the boil and then simmering 1 teaspoon of ripened quince seeds in 250 ml of distilled water for 15 minutes. Stir to prevent sticking. After the mixture has thickened to a gel, strain the seeds out.)

To keep your breath sweet and your mouth tasting fresh, you can try this herbal mouthwash: place 2 teaspoons of dried sage and 1 teaspoon each of dried peppermint and rosemary in a ceramic bowl and cover with 2 cups of boiling water. Add ½ cup of brandy or cider vinegar, cover the bowl and steep for 2 hours. Strain through fine muslin and then drip through coffee filter paper. Store in a tightly sealed bottle.

Use this mouthwash as a soothing gargle or as a refreshing rinse, as needed.

Remember, correct gum care means a healthy mouth and sweet breath. If plaque isn't removed daily, it eventually builds up causing gum disease — inflammation, swelling and bleeding are the first signs of gingivitis.

ORGANIC PEST CONTROL

Pests need to be controlled, but not totally eradicated. For many years we have been told that chemicals are the only method of effective pest control. However, good housekeeping practices combined with safe, natural, organic methods will help to control the problem without harming people or the environment.

Most natural methods of insect control tend to repel rather than kill, and occasionally more specific remedies may be needed, such as organic baits or sprays, which will break down quickly and

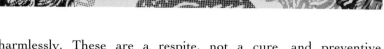

harmlessly. These are a respite, not a cure, and preventive methods must also be implemented.

It is far easier to: simply install insect screens; adjust household temperatures so that we do not provide a warm haven for insects to breed in; wipe up kitchen spills; keep the compost bin well sealed; and keep animal feed sealed in airtight containers. If insect pests do invade your living space and become an annoyance, the following methods will help to keep them under control.

ANTS

Wherever possible, try to simply deter ants by sprinkling eucalyptus oil or crushed garlic cloves along their paths. Placing slices of lemon along their paths is also reputed to be an effective repellent, as is a mixture of bicarbonate of soda and black pepper.

If you must use a bait, first make sure that it is inaccessible to children and pets. Mix together 2 cups of sugar and 2 tablespoons of borax, then dissolve the mixture in 1 cup of water. Pour into jars loosely filled with cottonwool, pierce holes in the jar lids and locate wherever you find ants. Jam laced with derris (available from garden supply stores), camphor, citronella or pepper also makes an effective bait.

COCKROACHES

Repel cockroaches by sprinkling a mixture of 1 part sugar and 1 part borax in cracks, crevices, corners and dark places, under the sink, at the backs of cupboards and drawers, or anywhere cockroaches hide. A bait made from equal parts of honey and borax is also effective. Place on small pieces of paper and leave in strategic places, renewing until left untouched. Remember, baits will only be effective if there is no other accessible food around, for example dirty dishes, food scraps.

FLIES

Use screened windows and doors to prevent entry. Those flies that do occasionally beat the barriers can be taken care of with a

flyswat or a bait made of half a teaspoon of black pepper, 1 teaspoon of brown sugar and a teaspoon of cream. Mix thoroughly and place in small dishes in inconspicuous places, and renew every few days.

To repel flies, place a few drops of lavender oil on a number of lengths of cotton ribbon about a centimetre wide and long enough to reach the floor, then hang the ribbons in frequently used doorways that lead outside. Renew the oil as needed.

SILVERFISH

Mix together a bait of equal portions of borax, flour and sugar and leave in bottle lids or on small pieces of paper in corners, cupboards, drawers and shelves. Vacuuming regularly and wiping shelves liberally with a potent lavender oil will also deter them for up to twelve months.

See also Fly Repellents, Garden Senses and Insects.

PAINT

CLEANING BRUSHES

Water-based Paint

Dissolve 100 grams of washing soda in hot water and soak the brushes in it. Work the bristles occasionally to allow the solution to penetrate. Rinse in clean water.

Oil Paint

Follow the procedure for water-based paint, and then before rinsing clean, put a small quantity of pure soap flakes in the bottom of a tin, add a little hot water to form a soft, thick paste and work the brush around in it. Keep repeating the procedure with fresh soap, rinsing each time, until all traces of paint have been removed.

PAPER

PAPER MAKING

Making paper yourself is simple and easy, and is a great way to recycle old newspapers, scraps of wallpaper, computer print-outs or any other bits of paper you may find. You'll need the following equipment: a large basin; rubber gloves; kitchen blender (optional); several large squares of calico; 2 waterproof boards (approximately 45 cm square); 4 G-clamps (available from hardward stores); and a special paper-making frame called a deckle (available from hobby or craft shops).

To start, tear your paper into small pieces and soak in warm water overnight. The next day, for a fine textured finish, liquidise each 2½ teaspoons of pulp with 750 ml of water for fifteen seconds in a kitchen blender.

If you want to make notepaper, it will have to be treated to receive the ink in a process called 'sizing'. This can be done by mixing ¼ teaspoon of homemade starch (*see Starch*) with a little cold water and then mixing into the pulp. You may have to adjust the amount of starch, depending upon the quantity of pulp being used. As a general guide, the amount specified is sufficient for a 5-litre bucket of sodden paper.

Next, fill your basin with pulp to just below the rim and lay a piece of calico over one of the boards. Dip the deckle vertically into the basin, tilt to horizontal below the water, and raise slowly, keeping the frame horizontal. Remove the top deckle guide frame, tip bottom frame, containing the pulp, upside down and onto the calico-covered board. Press down firmly and evenly to remove excess water, then carefully lift off the deckle.

Cover the pulp with another square of calico and repeat the process until all the pulp has been used, then cover the last lot of pulp with calico, place the second waterproof board on top, affix G-clamps to each corner and tighten each one a little at a time to maintain even pressure. Keep tightening until you can no longer keep tightening the clamps. Leave for 30 minutes, then remove the clamps and carefully lift off each sheet of calico, placing the pressed paper on a flat board to dry. To prevent paper from curling, lay another board on top and leave until completely dry.

Note. It is best to carry out this procedure outdoors, since the pressing will expel quite a lot of water.

PAPER DECORATIONS

You can add fragrant herbs, flowers or potpourri to the pulp once it has been taken up with the deckle, but before it is turned onto the pressing board. Use only dried herbs and flowers.

SCENTED WRITING PAPER

How delightful it is to both send and receive a letter that, when opened, releases a charming scent. Scented paper can easily be made from any type of paper, either home-made or bought. Simply place a thin, flat muslin bag of your favourite dry potpourri or other highly aromatic herbs in a box of writing paper and envelopes. Seal the box and leave it in a cool place for at least six weeks, so that the paper will absorb the fragrance.

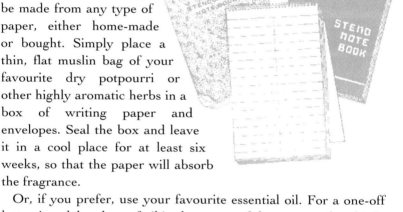

Or, if you prefer, use your favourite essential oil. For a one-off letter, just dab a drop of oil in the corner of the paper and seal it in the envelope. To scent a whole box of notepaper and envelopes, cut an old cotton handkerchief into small pieces, put a drop of essential oil on each piece and layer them between the sheets of paper. Seal the box tightly and leave for 24 hours.

Chose an oil that suits the mood or colour of the paper: lemon oil for yellow or cream-coloured paper, orange oil for peach-coloured, rose oil for pink, and so on.

See also Ink.

PERSPIRATION STAINS

See Lemon Juice.

PLASTIC

KITCHENWARE
Stains can be removed from plastic kitchenware by rubbing with a mixture of equal parts bicarbonate soda and coarse salt. Apply with a damp cloth and rinse clean.

ODOURS
Odours can be removed from plastic food containers by filling them with scrunched-up newspaper balls, and then placing them in the freezer for a few days.

To remove the taste and smell of plastic from the kids' plastic drink bottles, fill the bottles with a solution of bicarbonate of soda and warm water and allow to soak overnight. Rinse well with clean water.

STAINS
Plastic lunch boxes will give up even the most stubborn stain, and smell fresh, if you first soak them in a solution of bicarbonate of soda and water, and then scrub them with a damp cloth dipped in bicarbonate of soda.

PLAY DOUGH

This is the recipe my wife used to make play dough for our children when they were young.

Add the following ingredients, in the order they are listed, to a saucepan over a gentle heat and stir until well blended.

2 cups flour
2 cups warm water
2 tablespoons vegetable oil
2 tablespoons cream of tartar
1 cup salt

Keep stirring until the mixture is a pliable consistency, then remove from heat, place in a ceramic bowl and knead and punch it. Shape the dough into balls about the size of a closed fist.

Store the dough in the refrigerator in an airtight container so that it doesn't dry out.

POLISH

This liquid polish is ideal on all timber surfaces and will clean, polish and dust at the same time, with no need to buff afterwards.

Add 120 ml of linseed oil and 120 ml of malt vinegar to a bottle, seal tightly, and shake well to mix. Add 1 teaspoon of lemon oil and 1 teaspoon of lime oil or, if you prefer, add 1½ teaspoons of lavender oil and 4 drops of peppermint oil.

See also Cleaners (Timber Furniture Cleaner and Polish), Jasmine Furniture Polish, Lemon Timber Polish, and Polishing Cloth.

POLISHING CLOTH

To make a polishing cloth for cleaning timber surfaces, melt 15 grams of beeswax in a double boiler. When liquid, add 50 ml of white vinegar, stirring until thoroughly blended. Soak a cloth in this liquid for 15 minutes, squeeze it out and hang on the line to dry.

See also Cleaners (Timber Furniture Cleaner and Polish), Jasmine Furniture Polish, Lemon Timber Polish and Polish.

POMANDER

The origin of the pomander can be traced back to the ancient Greeks and the word 'pomander' is derived from the old French *pomme d'ambre*, or 'apple of amber'.

Early pomanders were mixtures of aromatic herbs and spices carried in perforated boxes or spheres of gold, silver or ivory. They were thought to ward off infection and allay unpleasant smells.

The homemade pomander, an orange studded with cloves, was first used by Cardinal Wolsey in the Middle Ages. He would take one with him whenever he visited his parishioners, holding it near his nose to counteract the stench of the streets.

You too can capture the delightful aroma of a traditional

pomander and keep wardrobes, cupboards and drawers fragrantly fresh all year round.

To make your pomander you will need:

1 large, thick-skinned orange
1 jar whole cloves
1 tablespoon freshly ground cinnamon
1 tablespoon orris root powder (from herb specialty shops and potpourri suppliers)

Gently knead the orange in your hands to soften the skin. Make a ring of holes around it with a wooden skewer, and press a clove into each hole. Continue to do this, working in circles towards one end, until the entire orange skin is covered.

Mix together the cinnamon and orris root powder. Roll the orange around in it until as much of the mixture as possible clings to it. Wrap the orange in tissue paper, place in a brown paper bag, and leave in a dry, dark, airy place for three to five weeks to cure. During this time, the orange will dry out completely and shrink slightly.

After the curing time, take the orange from the tissue and shake off any surplus powder. Your pomander is now ready for use. Place it in a drawer amongst precious woollens or delicate lingerie, or tie a ribbon around it and hang in a wardrobe. The scent should last for many years.

Pomanders also make effective moth deterrents, since household moths dislike the fragrance of cloves.

POTPOURRI

The potpourri is the traditional way to capture the wonderful fragrances of a summer herb garden all year round. The delightful aromatics of a potpourri can be used to gently perfume a room, cupboards, drawers and wardrobes, or can be stuffed into pillows to promote a blissful night's sleep.

Potpourri is the mixing of dried flower petals and herbs with certain fragrant ingredients and spices. Of course, you can use a store-bought potpourri, yet there is nothing quite as satisfying and pleasing as capturing those beautiful fragrances from your own garden for year-round enjoyment. The host of combinations that

you can concoct is limited only by your imagination, creativeness, and the flowers and herbs available.

To perfume your home with fragrant magic is simple. In a large ceramic bowl, mix together all the dry ingredients, using your hands to ensure a thorough mix. Add appropriate essential oils one drop at a time, mixing in well after each addition and testing for scent. Make sure you note down your favourite combinations for future reference.

Put the potpourri mix in a well-sealed plastic bag and leave to cure in a dry, dark spot for six weeks. Be sure to give the mix a good shake every second day.

Blends to try:

Marigold and Mint

½ cup dried thyme
½ cup peppermint leaves
1 cup dried marigold petals
4 drops peppermint oil
½ cup orris root powder (available from herb specialty shops and potpourri herb suppliers)

Rose Potpourri

6 cups dried rose petals
1 teaspoon dried mint leaves
1 teaspoon ground cloves
1 teaspoon ground cinnamon
1 teaspoon ground allspice
3 tablespoons orris root powder
6 drops rose oil

QUINCE

The quince is both an unusual and beautiful fruit-bearing tree and, if space and climate permits, deserves a spot in the garden. It will grow to around 4 metres tall with branches that grow in a most charmingly crooked manner. The blossoms are white or pale pink and are followed by an apple or pear-shaped fruit, which is extremely sweet-smelling when ripe.

The seeds from the ripened fruit can be used to make a gel which is valuable as a base for home-made cosmetics; alternatively, the fruit can be made into delicious quince jam. Recipes for both are given below.

QUINCE GEL

Add one teaspoon of seeds from a ripened quince to an enamel or stainless steel saucepan containing 250 ml of distilled water or herb water (see below). Bring slowly to the boil and simmer gently for about 15 minutes, stirring to prevent sticking. The mixture will thicken into a gel. Strain off the seeds and save in the refrigerator — they can be used several times.

Prepare a herbal infusion with your chosen herb (see list overleaf for suggestions) and use this rather than distilled water when making your quince gel, if desired.

To make a herbal infusion add 1 teaspoon of dried herb or 2 tablespoons of fresh herb of your choice to a ceramic bowl and cover with 300 ml of boiling water. Cover the bowl, steep overnight, strain through muslin cloth and use 250 ml for making your quince gel.

You now have a base to make your own natural facial cleanser, which can be adapted to your particular skin type.

Facial Cleanser
2 tablespoons quince gel
fine ground oatmeal

For your cleanser, mix sufficient oatmeal with the quince gel to form a paste. Rub over the face and neck, leave for five minutes, then rinse off with tepid water.

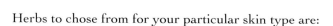

Herbs to chose from for your particular skin type are:

CAMOMILE	all skin types (including disturbed and sensitive skin)
ELDERFLOWER	all skin types (including sensitive skin)
LAVENDER	disturbed or oily skin
LEMONGRASS	disturbed or dry skin
CALENDULA	normal, oily and disturbed skin
ROSE PETALS	all skin types (including sensitive skin)
ROSEMARY	oily and disturbed skin
THYME	normal and disturbed skin
YARROW	oily and disturbed skin

QUINCE JELLY

3 kg quinces
400 g sugar to each 500 ml of juice

Cut the quinces into small pieces, but do not peel or core them. Put them in a large saucepan, cover with water and simmer until the fruit is soft and pulpy. Strain through a jelly (muslin) bag and leave to drip overnight — do not try and assist the process by squeezing the bag under any circumstances, or the quince jelly will be cloudy. Measure the juice and pour into a saucepan, then add 400 grams of sugar for every 500 ml of juice. Add to the saucepan and warm the juice until the sugar has dissolved, then boil fiercely until it begins to set. Fill clean, warm jars with the jelly, allow to cool, then seal.

Quince seeds contain plenty of pectin, so setting will not be a problem.

The jelly is delicious on toast for breakfast or as a relish with cold meats or chicken.

RASHES

Itchiness from a heat rash, allergy rash, nettle rash, or a rash that results from a viral infection may be relieved by applying a paste made from bicarbonate of soda and water. Itchy heat rash can be relieved by soaking in a tepid bath in which has been dissolved a half a cup of salt and a half a cup of vinegar.

RATS

Even a few tiny mice running around inside the roof can sound like a cavalry of giant rodents, but rats will have you ready to bring out the heavy artillery. They are more than just a nuisance; they are pests and they spread disease.

You can discourage any rodent from entering your house by scattering fresh or dried spearmint or peppermint around, or by placing small containers full of mixtures made from spearmint or peppermint essential oil. Perfume is the strongest formulation and should consist of 15 to 30 ml of essential oil to every 100 ml of water. So that the oil will completely emulsify with the water, dilute it in an equal quantity of methylated spirits first. Placing small containers of this mixture strategically around the house and roof should discourage these pests from turning your residence into theirs.

If you have rats in the house, their entry is usually evident by holes chewed through walls, ceilings and doors. Finding a mousehole might not be so easy. Sprinkle baking powder in front of suspect openings at night; next morning their tracks will be seen if they have been there.

Once rodents have gained access, no deterrent will keep them from their favourite meal. Traps placed along runways and other haunts have always been an effective means of control. If you feel too squeamish about using traps, a non-chemical bait provides an alternative to the usual poisons yet, like their counterparts, send the rodents away to die.

To make your bait, combine half a cup of cornflour and half a cup of plaster of Paris and mix to a dough with milk. Place small amounts in containers near entrance holes or runways.

REFRIGERATOR

CLEANING

See Cleaners (All Purpose Cleaner, Vinegar and Bicarbonate of soda)

ODOURS

Two or three sprigs of spearmint kept in a glass jar of water in the refrigerator eliminates smells. And to deodorise your refrigerator after cleaning, place an open packet of bicarbonate of soda inside of it. This will keep it smelling fresh for up to three months.

After cleaning the inside of your refrigerator wipe the inside, including door seals, with white vinegar to prevent mould from forming.

RELAXATION

In today's hectic world, stress and tension can have a severe toll upon your health and wellbeing. It will show up drastically in your face, causing tight muscles, wrinkles and a loss of skin tone.

Learn to relax: set aside a little time for yourself each day to do absolutely nothing. Stare into space, watch the waves at the beach, or watch the wind in the trees. In fact do anything that allows you to 'switch off'.

Exercise is one of the best natural stress busters. Go for a long walk, cycle or swim. Remember, any exercise will help you to relax and release built-up tension. If you don't have the chance to exercise — for instance, if you're at the office — sit back and take a few deep breaths. Breathe in deeply through your nose and out again several times, and this will help you to calm down.

Another effective yet simple way to unwind is to relax the muscles of your face, because when your face is relaxed, the rest of your body tends to follow. You can relax tense forehead muscles by gently massaging in a drop of eucalyptus oil with the tips of your fingers. Be careful not to rub anywhere near your eyes. By relaxing your lower jaw and your shoulders, you will aid the rest of the muscles in your body to relax.

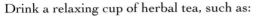

Drink a relaxing cup of herbal tea, such as:

LEMON BALM	a flavour of lemon and tangy mint
CAMOMILE	very soothing; sip slowly and relax
PEPPERMINT	very refreshing and calming
BASIL AND BORAGE	use twice as much borage as basil to make a relaxing and soothing tea
LEMON VERBENA	cooling in hot weather; has a sedative effect

See also Sleep.

RUST

CARS

To remove rust spots, rub the affected area with a piece of crumpled aluminium foil.

KETTLES

To prevent rust build-up in a metal kettle, simply leave two marbles inside it at all times.

TOOLS

To prevent rust on hand tools that are used infrequently or that you plan to store away, wipe over with an oily cloth then smear liberally with Vaseline.

BATHS AND SINKS

Rust stains on bathroom enamel can be removed by rubbing with a cloth dipped in white vinegar.

CLOTHING

Soak clothing with rust stains in a strong solution of lemon juice and salt. Leave in the sun to dry, then wash as normal.

SAGE

In the Middle Ages, the herb sage was believed to prolong life, heighten the spirits, keep away toads, avert chills, and enable girls to see their future husbands.

Today, we know that this universal herb can be used as a hair rinse and tonic, a mouthwash to keep teeth white, a treatment to alleviate rheumatism, a companion plant to help repel white cabbage moth and, of course, in salads, poultry stuffing, punches and cheese dishes.

Rub a fresh sage leaf on your teeth and watch it take away the plaque! Taken as a tea, sage will help people who sweat too much; it will alleviate wind and cramps; strengthen the stomach; aid in the elimination of worms in children; and even dry up milk in breastfeeding mothers.

When used as a gargle it is a remedy for sore throats and laryngitis, and when blended with brandy or cider vinegar it makes an ideal mouthwash for sweetening the breath.

Cold sage tea can be applied as an astringent tonic to the skin after cleansing, helping to close large facial pores. When used as a final hair rinse it will help prevent hair from going grey.

OILY SKIN TONIC

Put 3 tablespoons of dried sage in a ceramic bowl. Mix together 300 ml of cider vinegar and 300 ml of distilled water, and, in an enamel or stainless steel pan, heat to just below boiling point. Pour the liquid over the herbs, cover tightly with plastic wrap and leave to steep for 12 hours. Strain and bottle for future use.

Apply by gently dabbing the lotion onto cleansed skin with a cotton ball, and then leave to dry. Finish off with a moisturiser.

SALT

SALT IN THE DIET

Salt, one of the most commonly used natural food additives, can be dangerous to health if used excessively. It can cause stiffening of the joints, arthritis, hardening of the arteries and kidney disease. If it is taken in high enough concentrations, it will inhibit cell metabolism, and can eventually cause the death of cells.

Most people do not realise that the amount of salt the body needs — between 0.5 to 1 gram a day — can be found naturally in fish, meat, vegetables and grains. Too many individuals are consuming as much as 8 to 12 grams of salt every day by eating fast or convenience foods, or by adding it to meals at the dining table. You should avoid:

* salty snacks such as crisps, pretzels and salted nuts;
* too much take-away food;
* preserved meats;
* adding salt to your cooking; and
* putting the salt shaker on the table.

Nowadays, it is possible to buy many low-salt or salt-free foods ranging from canned food, butter and margarine, bread, breakfast cereals and much more. Gradually purchasing and using more of these types of food and adding herbs rather than salt to your cooking will help to wean your taste buds off salt. Many herbs will add flavours to your cooking that are very similar to salt.

A salt substitute made from herbs is a great way to add flavour to your food as well as providing essential vitamins and minerals. But like all condiments, it should be used with discrimination so as to not to overpower the natural flavour of the food.

Salt Substitute

1 tablespoon toasted sesame seeds
1 tablespoon yeast flakes
1 teaspoon celery seed, dried and ground
1 teaspoon garlic, dried and ground
½ teaspoon dill seed, dried and ground
2 cups parsley, dried and ground
1 teaspoon oregano, dried and ground
3 strips lemon peel, dried and ground
1 teaspoon thyme, dried and ground
1 teaspoon coriander seed, dried and ground

First, finely grind together the sesame seeds and the yeast flakes. Thoroughly mix together the remaining ingredients and mix well

with the sesame seeds and yeast flakes. Pass through a fine wire sieve and store in an airtight jar. Label and date the jar and use within twelve months. It can be added to cooking and used at the table instead of salt.

SALT AS A CLEANING AGENT

Drains
To clear and clean a drain, put a handful of salt in the drain and follow this with 2 litres of boiling water.

Cookware
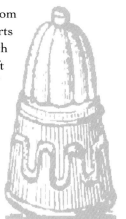

To clean copper pans and copper-bottom pans, scrub with a mixture of 2 parts vinegar and 1 part salt. Rinse off with hot water and polish dry with a soft cloth. Enamel saucepans, especially if brown, can be cleaned by simply scouring with coarse salt, then washing in hot soda water.

Kitchen Surfaces
Salt has excellent disinfectant properties and is ideal for scouring sinks and chopping boards used for food preparation.

SANDFLY BITE

Apply undiluted lavender oil as soon as possible after being bitten.

SAUNAS

Two drops of pine or eucalyptus oil added to a ladle of water, or 15 drops to a small bucket, make an acceptable and antiseptic inhalant in saunas. It is also ideal for stuffy heads from cold, flu and sinusitis.

SCENTED WRITING PAPER

See Ink and Paper (Scented Writing Paper).

SCRATCHES

See Cuts and Abrasions, and Tea Tree Oil.

SEAWEED FERTILISER

See Garden Fertilisers.

SEPTIC TOILETS

Throwing 1 cup of bicarbonate of soda down a septic toilet each week will clean the toilet, reduce acidity, and encourage the growth of waste-digesting bacteria.

SINK

CLEANING SINKS

See Salt (Salt as a Cleaning Agent).

SINUSITIS

See Anise, Hay Fever and Tea Tree Oil.

SKIN

MAINTAINING HEALTHY SKIN

Beautiful skin can be a lifelong asset, but needs to be cherished, protected and maintained. Cleansing and moisturising will counteract the drying, chapping and roughening effects of the wind, sun and other environmental conditions, and will help speed up the skin's renewal process.

It is important to consider both the type of cleanser you use and the lotion you use to help replenish the natural oils taken away by cleansing. However, the skin must also be nourished from within to maintain proper health. In order for your skin to be glowing, your body needs a good balance of vitamins, minerals, herbs and amino acids. As well as being important to the functions of the body in general, vitamins B_3, B_5 and B_6 are vital to the health of your skin. Zinc also plays an important role by assisting in the healing process and increasing your resistance to skin eruptions;

vitamin A helps the skin to retain moisture and keeps it in good condition; and vitamin C assists in the formation and elasticity of tissue, and in skin repair. They are available as supplements from your local health-food store but, where possible, include your daily intake of essential vitamins and minerals in a well-balanced diet.

Herbs and foods such as alfalfa, dandelion, burdock, parsley, sage, wheatgerm, peanuts, brewers' yeast, unpolished rice and soya beans will help to provide the essential B group vitamins, and for vitamin C there is, of course, oranges. Green and red peppers are also a good source of vitamin C, as are brussels sprouts, blackcurrant juice, watercress, dandelion greens and tropical fruits such as rockmelons, mangoes and pawpaws. Yellow and orange vegetables are a good source of vitamin A, as is sweet potato and herbs such as alfalfa, burdock, cayenne, dandelion greens, parsley and watercress. Dandelion exceeds all other greens on the market in vitamin A content by at least four times. Zinc can be found in foods such as kelp, the herb marshmallow, oysters, lean beef, lean pork, brown rice, salmon, fish, crabs and lobsters.

Nourishing the Skin
To keep your skin looking healthy and supple, the regular use of a nourishing lotion after a bath or shower is essential.

A simple moisturising lotion can be made by blending together 50 ml of glycerine, 75 ml of rose-water, 45 ml of almond oil, 20 ml of wheatgerm oil, 5 ml of jojoba oil, 12 drops of rose essential oil and 8 drops of oil of frankincense (optional). Place in an amber-coloured glass bottle which is tightly sealed, and shake well to thoroughly mix all ingredients.

Apply generously, massaging well into the skin.

See also Cucumber Cold Cream, Herbal Skin Care and Lavender.

Protection

Wind, cold weather, air conditioning and the sun can all dry and damage the skin. Protection is a must, and can be simply achieved with natural home-made preparations.

To prevent facial skin and hands from becoming dry, scaly, chapped or split, apply the following moisturising lotion every morning and night, or whenever required. It will keep your skin soft and supple.

Mix 20 grams of ground almonds and 3 drops of rose oil with 500 ml of distilled water and allow to stand for 1 hour. Strain through fine muslin, add half a teaspoon of sugar and 6 drops of friar's balsam (tincture of benzoin, available from pharmacies) and stir until the sugar has dissolved. Bottle and seal.

CHAPPED SKIN

For skin that is already chapped, make up the following oil and massage over the affected area. Blend 10 drops of rose oil, 10 drops of camomile oil, 5 drops of lemon oil and 5 drops of lavender oil with 30 ml of almond oil. Store in an amber-coloured glass bottle away from direct heat or sunlight, and use within two months.

Chapped and sore lips can be treated by applying a mixture of 2 drops of camomile oil, 2 drops of geranium oil and 2 teaspoons of aloe vera juice (available from health-food stores).

For cold sores, put 1 drop of either tea tree or camomile oil on a cotton bud and apply it directly to the sore as soon as it appears. Repeat every day.

See also Chapped Lips.

SLEEP

We all need regular, restful and sound sleep to keep healthy. Sleep allows the mind and body to unwind and restores lost energy. Yet all of us at some time have one of those nights where we just can't go to sleep: tossing and turning and reliving every single facet of the day's activities. Fatigue, tension, anxiety, over-excitement or pain are some of the causes of an occasional sleepless night.

If you can't sleep, ask yourself why. Do you tend to overwork every day? Do you feel almost too exhausted to get ready for bed? If the answer is yes, you are creating a vicious cycle of overtiredness: the inability to relax and regenerate at night causes you even more fatigue the next day, and so on. Re-examine your daytime activities and establish a natural rhythm that allows your body to relax.

Of course, overwork may not always be the problem. If you feel your daily habits are not causing excessive fatigue so that you are unable to have a restful night's sleep, look at your sleeping environment. Is your bed comfortable? Does it sag in the middle? Is your mattress rock hard? Are your bed clothes too heavy? All are contributing factors in preventing you from having a restful night's sleep.

Choose a bed that is comfortable, yet firm, and will provide adequate support for your spine.

Sufficient fresh air at night and an adequate diet are also important. Stuffy rooms will leave you feeling jaded in the morning, will dehydrate the skin, and can cause accumulation of fluid around the eyes, making

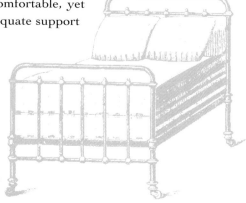

them baggy when you awake. Also, check your diet. If you are one of those 'one-in-four Australians' who continually suffers from insomnia, you may not be getting sufficient vitamins and minerals to soothe jangled nerves and tone up the nervous system. If your diet is not adequate, take a daily supplement, available from health-food stores, to ensure a balanced calcium and magnesium intake. Include the following foods in your diet: apples, avocadoes, barley, almonds, cabbage, celery, sweet-corn, lettuce, fresh sliced mushrooms, onions, spring onions, green peas, baked potatoes, brown rice, soya beans and tomatoes.

Herbal teas which are soothing and strengthening to the nerves can be taken after dinner, instead of coffee, and half an hour before going to bed. Camomile is an excellent choice and is readily available; it will soothe both the nerves and an overactive and tired brain, helping to promote sound, natural sleep.

If you have had a really hectic day or are feeling over-tired and fatigued, relax with your cup of herbal tea and then completely unwind in a soothing herbal bath. Put 2 tablespoons of dried camomile in the centre of a 20 square cm of muslin or cheesecloth. Draw up the sides and secure them with a piece of ribbon, then hang the herb bag under the running tap so that the hot water gushes through it.

A blend of essential oils added to your bath instead of the herbs will also help you to unwind and relax. Blend 2 drops of camomile oil and 2 drops of rose oil with 6 drops of lavender oil and then mix thoroughly with 30 ml of almond oil. Store the oil in an airtight, amber-coloured glass bottle, and add about 10 drops of oil to your bath while the taps are running, whenever required.

When finally retiring, remove all external disturbances such as a ticking clock or a humming electrical machine. You may also try changing the lightbulb in your bedside table lamp to a low-voltage, soothing coloured one. Excellent colours are light shades of pink and green. Make sure you have good ventilation in your bedroom, because stuffiness is often the cause of waking in the night.

To ensure that you sleep the whole night through, put a drop of basil, camomile, clary sage, juniper or lavender oil onto your pillow at night.

See also Dill Water.

SMELLING SALTS

Smelling salts make a useful addition to the bathroom cabinet. To relieve a stuffy nose or a headache, simply hold the smelling salts under your nose.

To make your smelling salts, fill a small, amber-coloured bottle with coarse sea salt. Add 1 teaspoon of friar's balsam (tincture of benzoin, available from pharmacies) and 1 teaspoon of mandarin, tangerine, orange or lemon essential oil.

See also Vinaigrette.

SOAP

See Herbal Soap.

SOAP SCRAPS

Those little slivers of soap that end up in the bottom of the shower recess or the bathroom sink can be very annoying. Don't throw them out! Instead, save and recycle them into useful household soap products.

HANDY CLEANING GEL

Soap scraps can be made into a handy cleaning gel for general household and laundry use. This gel will remove most stubborn stains and is excellent for removing grease from carpets and for washing greasy clothes. Place soap scraps in a saucepan, cover with water and allow to soak for 24 hours, stirring occasionally. Bring to boil over a medium heat, stirring continuously, then reduce to a simmer. Whisk or mash to completely dissolve the soap. Remove from heat, allow to cool, and for each cup of the resultant soap-like jelly, add 2 cups of talcum powder and 2 tablespoons of mineral turpentine. Mix well and store in a large, wide-mouthed container with a tight-fitting lid.

ALL-PURPOSE STAIN REMOVER

For an all-purpose stain remover, mix together, in an enamel or stainless steel saucepan, 4 cups of finely grated or chopped soap scraps, 3 tablespoons of eucalyptus oil, 1 cup of methylated spirits and 1 cup of boiling water.

Stand the saucepan in a larger pan of hot water over a medium heat, stirring the mixture until it turns clear. Pour into moulds (empty milk cartons are ideal) and leave to cool and set. Cut into bars and leave for about four weeks to fully harden.

ROSE PETAL SOAP

Designed for personal use, this fragrant rose petal soap is both mild and softening to the skin. Put 10 tablespoons of finely grated soap scraps in a saucepan, cover with water and soak for 24 hours, stirring occasionally.

Crush 2 tablespoons of dried rose petals and reduce them to a powder by rubbing through a fine wire sieve.

Bring the soap mixture to the boil, stirring until the soap is dissolved. Remove from heat and for each cupful add 1 tablespoon of almond oil. Then add the powdered rose petals and stir thoroughly to blend. Add rose oil (optional), drop by drop, until sufficiently scented. Pour the mixture into moulds (empty milk cartons are ideal) and leave to cool and set, then cut into bars. Allow the soap to harden for two weeks before using.

HONEY AND OATMEAL SOAP

Place 2 cups of grated soap scraps in a saucepan, cover with cold water and allow to stand for 24 hours. Add 2 tablespoons of honey and simmer, stirring occasionally, until the soap has melted. Remove from heat, stir in a half a cup of oatmeal and 2 tablespoons of glycerine, mixing well. Pour into moulds (empty milk cartons are ideal) and leave to cool and set, then cut into bars. Allow the soap bars to cure for about six weeks before using.

See also Herbal Soap.

SOLAR ELECTRICITY

See Energy Efficient Homes.

SORE THROAT

See Honeysuckle and Tea Tree Oil.

SPLINTERS

An easy way to ensure the straightforward, pain free extraction of a splinter is to first apply olive oil to the area.

SPLIT LIPS

See Chapped Lips and Skin.

SPRAINS

See Witch Hazel Ointment.

STARCH

SPRAY-ON STARCH

This spray-on starch can be used to spray on garments whilst ironing, and if perfumed with an aromatic herb, will give your clothes a delightful fragrance.

2 teaspoons dried lavender (or fragrant herb of choice)
600 ml boiling water
10 ml methylated spirits
½ teaspoon gum tragacanth (available from pharmacies)

Put the dried herb in a ceramic bowl and pour in the boiling water. Cover, steep overnight, and strain through muslin cloth, squeezing all liquid from the herbs. Warm the infusion and dissolve the gum tragacanth, then stir in sufficient powdered starch to make a viscous, creamy liquid. Add the methylated spirits, stirring until it is completely blended, and store in a pump-spray bottle.

See Laundry Sense (Starch).

STEEL WOOL

See Horsetail.

STINGS AND BITES

Mosquito and ant bites can be relieved by the application of a paste made from bicarbonate of soda and water.

For bee and wasp stings, make a thick paste of bicarbonate of soda and water, apply to the affected area, then cover with a cold wet cloth. With a bee sting, you must first remove the actual stinger before treating with the soothing agent.

See also Bee Stings and Mosquito Bites.

SUEDE SHOES

To remove stains on suede shoes, cover with cornstarch and brush off after a few minutes, then hold over a steaming kettle, afterwards brushing well with a suede brush.

SUMMER COOLING

Did you know that trees are natural air conditioners? It's always cool beneath a tree because their leaves block out solar radiation and release water into the air. Deciduous trees planted in front of north-facing house walls create the maximum amount of shade to cool the house in summer, whilst still allowing sunlight to penetrate and warm the house in winter. When planting trees that will eventually grow quite large, make sure that they are situated far enough away from the house so that growing branches and roots won't become a problem.

Trees may also be planted to channel cool breezes to the house in summer, and will also deflect cold winds away in winter. The good old Australian verandah will not only protect the walls from sun and rain, but will provide a cool, shady outdoor living area in hot weather. Your veranda can be fitted with screens to give protection from biting insects.

Temperature control can be as simple as growing deciduous vines, such as grape or wisteria, over a pergola — a sensible, natural solution to cooling, given the high angle of the sun in the summer sky.

Attached shadehouses made of lattice and shade cloth also offer a cool retreat from soaring summer temperatures. Vines can be grown over the outside of the shadehouse and plants hung on the inside. Light will filter through the greenery and the hanging plants will help to lower the surrounding temperature.

To reduce the amount of heat coming through your windows and sliding doors make sure they are all fitted with curtains, blinds or shutters. To work effectively they must be well sealed on the bottom and sides, and on the top by a pelmet.

External shades, such as roll-up awnings, can be very effective. Individual window pergolas covered in vines or creepers not only block out summer sun, but will give the inside of your house a cool, greenish, broken light.

The window pergola need be no more than an extended window box with individual lengths of wire running from it to the top of the window frame. In hot areas where you wish to block out the sun all year round evergreens like passionfruit are suitable, while if you want to receive winter sunlight, deciduous vines such as grapes are more appropriate.

Instead of investing in an energy-hungry air-conditioning unit, consider installing a revolving ceiling fan. They freshen and circulate the air inside your house and cool your body by encouraging the moisture on your skin to evaporate. Consider a solar fan which runs on a small electric motor powered directly by a solar cell panel.

When the sun begins to set, your house can be cooled by cross-ventilation. To gain the maximum benefit from cool breezes, your house should have smaller, low-level openings on the windward side. By having larger openings on the other side, cool breezes will be channelled through the house. Your house need not face directly into the breeze, as long as it is offset by no more than 45 degrees. If so, a row of shrubs, or a high fence, will redirect the breeze.

SUN PROTECTION

To avoid premature aging of the skin, wrinkles and the possibility of skin cancer, it is essential to wear a sunscreen, and keep as covered up as possible, when exposed to the sun. Cool, long-sleeve cotton shirts or blouses and slacks are a must, and are also very comfortable in hot weather. Don't forget to wear a suitable, wide-brimmed hat.

If you do get caught out in the sun and suffer sunburn, it is important to drink plenty of fluids and herb teas, such as rosemary and lemongrass. To ease the stinging and pain of sunburn, use any of the following first-aid measures:

* Apply the juice of an aloe vera leaf straight onto the affected area. Waterlily leaves and stems will also give relief.
* Dab milk or yoghurt onto the skin.
* Lay thin slices of cucumber on the skin to ease the stinging.
* Cover the affected skin with a paste made from bicarbonate of soda and water.

Cases of severe sunburn should always be referred to your health practitioner.

Sun Toner

This lotion is not designed for sunburnt skin, but is excellent for counteracting the dehydrating effects of the sun.

Blend together 50 ml of rose-water, 50 ml of witch hazel solution (available from pharmacies, health-food stores and some super-markets) and 100 ml of distilled water, and store in a spray bottle. Spray on skin as desired, avoiding contact with the eyes.

You will find that this toner is slightly astringent, leaving your skin feeling cool and delightfully fragrant.

See also Honeysuckle (Honeysuckle Ointment) and Witch Hazel Ointment.

TEA (HERBAL)

See Drinks (Herbal), Indigestion and Sleep.

TEA TREE OIL

The antiseptic action of the oil of the tea tree (*Melaleuca alternifolia*) is considered to be 10 times more powerful than carbolic acid — and yet in small doses it is non-poisonous to humans! Australian Aborigines have long made use of this native tree in their medications. Its anti-viral, anti-fungal and anti-bacterial properties make it useful in treating a whole range of first aid situations as well as other minor problems: infections, sunburn, acne, athlete's foot, toothache and gum disease, to name but a few.

Commercially, tea tree oil is used in body lotions, toilet soaps, skin washes and for many other household applications.

A bottle in the bathroom cabinet is a must for those emergency first-aid situations. Use it for the following:

* For abrasions, cuts and scratches, wash the wound thoroughly and apply tea tree oil two or three times daily with a clean cotton-wool ball. Two or three drops in a bowl of warm water makes an excellent antiseptic wash.

* Apply tea tree oil to relieve the itchiness and irritation of mosquito stings and other insect bites.

* For temporary relief of muscular aches and pains, blend 6 drops of tea tree oil with 10 ml of olive oil and apply before and after exercise. To make the oil penetrate even better, add 10 drops of avocado oil to the blend, mixing thoroughly. A teaspoon of oil added to a hot bath will also help to relieve muscular aches and pains.

* To treat minor burns, first flush the affected area of skin with cold water, then apply undiluted tea tree oil.

* When suffering from a head cold, sinusitis, or bronchial or nasal congestion, dilute 1 teaspoon of tea tree oil in a basin of hot water and use as an inhalation. Hold your face about 30 cm away from the basin and cover your head with a towel large enough to make a tent and inhale the vapours for around

ten minutes. People with heart and blood pressure problems, asthma or other breathing difficulties, broken skin or visible, diluted red veins, should avoid using steam inhalations, unless otherwise directed by their health practitioner.

* Apply immediately to cold sores when they first appear, and use 3–4 times daily for up to, but no more than, five days.
* For a persistent sore throat, add 4 drops of tea tree oil to 25 ml warm water and gargle two to three times daily.
* Tea tree lotion will give soothing relief to dry skin, cracked heels, sunburn and other skin irritations, including shaving rash, and nappy rash and chafe. To help clear pimples and kill bacteria, apply three times a day.
* Tea tree oil can also be used to treat the family pet for flea and tick bites, eczema and mange. Mix 5–10 drops of tea tree oil in with the lather when you shampoo your pet and leave on for a few minutes before rinsing.

TERRAZZO

Stubborn stains can be removed from terrazzo tiles with a cut lemon dipped in salt. Rub the lemon well into the area, leave for an hour, then mop over with a solution of 1 cup of vinegar and half a bucket of water.

THYME

Thyme has a haunting sweet aroma, particularly noticeable when you brush against the leaves or tread on the plant when it is growing between paving stones.

During the Middle Ages, thyme was given by a lady to her beloved Knight as a farewell gift when he embarked on the crusades, and Knights who ate thyme were thought to become more courageous.

Thyme is a powerful antiseptic, rich in thymol, and has many cosmetic benefits. It acts as an astringent and helps to clear spots and acne, it cleanses, soothes and refreshes the skin, and when added to bath water as a strong infusion, it is excellent for skin problems. As a scent herb, it is used in sachets, as a moth

repellent, in rubbing vinegars, in bath lotions, in bags for herbal baths, in perfumed soap, and in potpourri.

A cooled tea made from thyme makes an excellent mouthwash to freshen the breath and is reputed to calm a cough and get rid of phlegm. Make a tea by infusing a few sprigs of thyme in hot water, or use a proprietary brand herbal tea bag available from health-food stores and supermarkets. If you use fresh thyme, choose culinary, Westmoreland or lemon thyme.

The oil of this herb is one of the strongest antiseptics known and, therefore, thyme tea is reputed to also be helpful as an antiseptic for infected wounds, and to treat fungal problems such as athlete's foot.

Culinary thyme (*Thymus vulgaris*) is traditionally used in cooking and is an essential ingredient in the classic 'bouquet garni', which imparts its special taste to casseroles, soups and sauces. This thyme is always the choice of French chefs, and is easily grown in pots in out-of-the-way spots around the garden. To make a bouquet garni, simply tie together in a small bunch, with a piece of cotton, two sprigs of thyme, one sprig of parsley and a bay leaf.

Thyme in herb bread gives it a delicious, mouth-watering flavour. A few fresh leaves sprinkled over cooked vegetables makes them just that little bit more appetising.

Westmoreland thyme (*Thymus serpyllum Westmoreland*), although milder, is also a wonderful variety for culinary purposes, with a fine flavour and fragrance.

Lemon thyme, with its refreshing citrus overtones, is good with fish, chicken and other white meats, and is a must in mornays and omelettes. For an extra taste sensation, blend with tarragon, chives, chervil and parsley.

Put several sprigs of your favourite thyme in a cup of cooking oil or cider vinegar and leave to infuse, in a sunny spot, for a few weeks. Use this fragrant oil or vinegar as a baste when barbecuing or when sautéing meats and vegetables. Lemon scented thyme oil makes an excellent fish baste. The vinegar can be used as a salad dressing to give that extra taste and zing.

THYME SLEEP MIXTURE

Dried thyme can be blended with other herbs in a potpourri mix that will help to promote sound, healthy sleep.

1 cup dried lemon thyme

1 cup dried lavender flowers

1 cup dried marjoram

1 teaspoon cinnamon

1 tablespoon dried orange peel, crumbled

1 tablespoon orris root powder

Mix all the ingredients together, put them in an airtight glass container and leave in a dark, warm cupboard for six weeks. Shake every other day to help cure the mixture. It is then ready to put into individual bags made of coarse cotton.

Stitch bags across the top once they have been filled with the herb mixture. Tuck into pillows for a restful night's sleep.

TICK REPELLENT

Make a mild tick repellent for both dogs and cats by mixing equal parts of eucalyptus oil, pennyroyal oil, thyme oil and olive oil. Comb this mixture through your pet's fur and renew weekly or when the scent is no longer noticeable.

TILES

Vinyl, slate, cork, ceramic and linoleum tiles can all be washed with a solution of 1 cup of vinegar and half a bucket of warm water. The vinegar will prevent any 'spotting' as the floor dries. For a disinfectant cleaner, add 5 ml of lavender oil to the solution, dissolving it in the vinegar first.

ULCERS

MOUTH

Mouth ulcers are caused by a minor viral infection and will usually respond to a mouthwash and ointment. However, persistent ulcers or acute problems should be referred to your health practitioner.

Mouth Wash
1 drop peppermint oil
1 drop geranium oil
1 drop thyme oil
2 drops lemon oil
5 ml brandy
250 ml (1 cup) distilled water

Dilute the essential oils in the brandy and then mix thoroughly with the water. Swish around inside the mouth several times but do not swallow.

Aloe Vera Ointment
20 ml aloe vera juice (available from health-food stores)
2 drops camomile oil
1 drop thyme oil

Blend the oils thoroughly with the aloe vera juice and store in the refrigerator in an airtight, amber-coloured glass bottle. Use within 3 days — if the mixture begins to smell rancid discard immediately and make a new batch.

Smooth a little of the ointment around the ulcerated area after using the mouthwash.

URINE

HUMAN
With young children, bedwetting is often a problem, and results in stained mattresses and sheets. Rinse sheets and pyjamas in cold, salted water, then wash as usual.

Mattresses need to be attended to straight away, as the urine can quite easily soak through to the stuffing. Cover the affected area immediately with a mixture of equal parts of powdered borax and kaolin (China clay), sprinkle on a few drops of lavender oil, cover with a thick towel and leave for two to three days. Vacuum up the powder, sponge the surface with white vinegar and leave in the sun to dry. If there is any residual smell, sprinkle on a few drops of lavender oil before making the bed — remember, lavender is a potent oil, so apply it sparingly.

VACUUM CLEANER

A teaspoon of the carpet deodorant powder (*see Carpet Deodoriser*) placed in the dust bag of your vacuum cleaner will stop the odour that builds up from dust and dirt. As the air is sucked through the vacuum cleaner, the aromatics of the powder will also fragrance the air.

Alternatively, add 8 drops of your favourite essential oil to a cotton-wool ball and place this in the dust bag. To vary the fragrance of your surroundings, place a new cotton-wool ball with a different oil in the vacuum cleaner every time your vacuum or empty the bag. Try oils like lemon, lavender or pine to eliminate the dusty feeling often associated with this household chore.

VACUUM FLASK

Vacuum flasks that have not been used for a while, and which have a staleness about them, can be freshened by half filling with warm water and adding 2 teaspoons of bicarbonate of soda. Replace lid, shake well, then top up with more warm water and allow to stand for twelve hours. Rinse with fresh water.

VINAIGRETTE

A vinaigrette is no more than a strong-scented herbal vinegar, usually kept in a special 'smelling bottle'. They were extremely popular in England in the early 1800s, being considered an essential accessory for fashionable young men and women meeting in crowded ballrooms and stuffy taverns.

Today, vinaigrettes make an ideal natural addition to the bathroom cabinet to relieve a stuffy nose or headache, and can be made as follows:

2 tablespoons dried lavender
2 tablespoons dried rosemary
1 tablespoon dried mint
1 tablespoon dried marjoram
150 ml cider vinegar

150 ml distilled water
1 teaspoon camphorated oil (available from pharmacies)

Put all the herbs in a ceramic bowl. Mix together the cider vinegar and distilled water, and heat in an enamel pan to just below boiling point. Pour the liquid over the herbs, cover tightly with plastic wrap and leave to steep for 24 hours. Strain, add the camphorated oil and mix well.

Push a small piece of natural sponge into a bottle. Pour in the vinegar liquid and seal tightly. Any leftover vinegar liquid can be bottled and used in the bath.

To use, remove the lid and hold the bottle under your nose. Breathe deeply to revive yourself if you are feeling faint, or to clear a stuffed-up nose.

See also Smelling Salts.

VIOLET CLEANSING MILK

This natural lotion is both soothing and cleansing to the skin as well as being gently astringent.

3 heaped teaspoons fresh violet petals
1½ cups milk

Put the violet petals in a ceramic bowl over a saucepan of hot water. Add the milk and heat to just below simmering point. Cover and leave over heat until the milk smells strongly of violets, stirring gently from time to time. Strain through muslin into a bottle with a tight-fitting lid. Keep in the refrigerator and use within three days.

Apply gently to facial skin with a cotton-wool ball in an upward and outward movement.

VITAMINS

Confusion with the variety and multiplicity of vitamins available from your pharmacy or health-food store may lead to you buying too many, too few, or products that are totally unsuitable for your needs. Multi-vitamin capsules are rarely the answer: each individual's needs are so different that you could still find yourself lacking in some essential vitamins.

Vitamin D is the only vitamin which is manufactured by your body; the rest must be absorbed from the food and drink you consume. Nearly all vitamins are manufactured by plants — a very good reason why you should eat plenty of vegetables and herbs to guarantee both freshness and freedom from chemicals.

A correct vitamin balance means good health both internally and externally: because you feel good, you look good and maintain a healthy glow.

Vitamins are the building blocks that make us into healthy, bounding-with-energy human beings. Select foods and herbs containing sufficient vitamins and include them in your diet each day to be assured of a correct vitamin balance. Remember, natural sources are always better than pills.

VITAMIN A

This vitamin cures skin diseases and keeps you looking good. Sources of vitamin A include yellow and orange vegetables, sweet potato, alfalfa, cayenne, dandelion greens, parsley and watercress.

B GROUP VITAMINS

These vitamins calm the nerves and ensure good health of the nervous and digestive systems; regulate and stabilise liver function; convert unsaturated fats into body fuel; protect natural hair colour, thus preventing premature greying; are useful in skin disorders; and help to soften wiry or tightly curled hair, making it more manageable. Sources of B group vitamins include: brewer's yeast, milk, cheese, whey, eggs, wheatgerm, rice bran, nuts, legumes, potatoes, unpolished rice, soya beans, peanuts, strawberries and dandelion.

VITAMIN C

This vitamin controls the tone and resilience of the body's cells, assists in repairing and renewing cells, and hardens the dentine of your teeth. It also carries hydrogen round the body, assisting the absorption of iron. Sources of vitamin C include rosehips, green and red peppers, brussels sprouts, guava, parsley, citrus fruits, sweet potato, rockmelon, mangoes, pawpaw, fresh red cabbage, kale and mustard greens.

Vitamin D

This vitamin enables calcium and phosphorus to be used by the body, regulates the metabolism, and is necessary for the health of your eyes. We rely upon the sun for our intake of vitamin D.

Vitamin E

Vitamin E improves overall body health, and stops other vitamins from being oxidised, so that they can be completely assimilated by the body in their pure state. Sources of vitamin E include wheatgerm (best and most available source), sunflower seeds, pumpkin seeds, beans, peas, soya oil, safflower oil and oatmeal.

Vitamin F

This vitamin controls your metabolic rate, takes care of your cholesterol balance, and prevents eczema and dull, dry hair. It can also play a role in the correction of dandruff and acne, and regulates over-activity of the sebaceous glands. Sources of vitamin F include: vegetable oils, fish (tuna, salmon, eel), rice, wheatgerm and most nuts (except cashews).

Vitamin K

Essential for the blood's clotting action. Sources of vitamin F include: green leafy vegetables such as spinach, cabbage, carrot tops and alfalfa, and soya bean and cod liver oil.

Vitamin P

Rutin, the major part of this vitamin, keeps blood vessels pumping efficiently, and has great therapeutic value for infections and diseases of the eye. Sources of vitamin P include buckwheat and the pulp (not just the juice) of lemons and oranges.

See also Diet, Herbs in the Diet, Minerals and Nutrition.

VOMITING

To ease vomiting, take frequent sips of strong, hot peppermint tea. Prepare the tea using 3 or 4 peppermint tea bags (available from health- food shops and supermarkets) in a cup of hot water. Infuse for five minutes and reheat if necessary.

See also Nausea.

WARTS

Choose one of the following and rub onto the wart morning and night until it disappears:

- ❋ freshly crushed marigold leaves (rub on)
- ❋ a few drops from a hollow dandelion stem
- ❋ cabbage leaf juice (use a juicer, or bruise cabbage leaves and squeeze out the juice)
- ❋ fresh pineapple juice
- ❋ wheatgerm oil.

WASH BAGS

See Kids.

WASHING CLOTHES

See Clothes, Eucalyptus Oil, Laundry Sense and Lavender Wool Wash.

WASHING MACHINES

See Laundry Sense.

WASP STING

Being alkaline, this type of sting is best treated with cider vinegar. Mix 2 drops of lavender oil, 2 drops of camomile oil and 5 ml (1 teaspoon) of cider vinegar, and dab on the affected area three times a day.

WEED SPRAY

Provided weeds and grasses are shallow-rooted, they can be eliminated from garden beds and from between pavers with a safe herbicide made from human urine. After collecting the urine, allow it to stand in a covered bucket for 24 hours or more before using. Apply using a pump-spray bottle to the leaves and base of weeds.

WHITEN CLOTHES

See Laundry Sense and Yellowing.

WITCH HAZEL OINTMENT

Use this soothing cream to ease aches, sprains and sunburn.

10 g beeswax
20 ml witch hazel solution (available from pharmacies)
20 ml rose-water
5 ml almond oil
60 ml hazel nut oil
6 drops friar's balsam (tincture of benzoin, available from pharmacies)

Melt the beeswax in a double boiler (enamel or stainless steel) over a medium heat. When completely melted add the witch hazel, rose-water and oils, stirring until completely blended. Remove from heat, allow to cool slightly, add the friar's balsam, and beat with a wooden spoon or electric mixer until cool and of a creamy texture. Store in an airtight, sterilised glass jar.

WOOD BETONY

An aromatic wild herb, wood betony *(Betonica officinalis)* resembles a small stinging nettle, and has dark green leaves and lilac-pink flowers. It is easily cultivated in the home garden, being adaptable to a wide range of conditions.

Wood betony makes an excellent substitute for regular tea, having a similar taste but being caffeine-free. It also makes a good general tonic, is said to be effective against worms, helps to alleviate hayfever, and can be made into an ointment for use on sprains, cuts and sores.

BETONY OINTMENT

4 tablespoons dried wood betony leaves
150 ml almond oil
5 g beeswax
10 g anhydrous lanolin
5 ml wheatgerm oil
20 ml distilled water
20 ml aloe vera juice
5 drops friar's balsam (tincture of benzoin,
available from pharmacies)

Add the wood Betony leaves and almond oil to an enamel or stainless steel saucepan, bring to the boil, and then reduce the heat and simmer for ten minutes. Remove from heat and strain.

In a double saucepan (enamel or stainless steel), melt the beeswax and lanolin over a medium heat until reduced to liquid. Warm 60 ml of the herbal almond oil and add it, along with the wheatgerm oil, distilled water and aloe vera juice, to the melted wax. Stir until well blended, remove from heat, allow to cool slightly and add the friar's balsam. Beat with a wooden spoon or electric mixer until cool and of a creamy texture. Store in a tightly capped, sterilised glass jar and use within three months.

WOOLLEN GARMENTS

See Clothes, Eucalyptus Oil, Laundry Sense, Lavender Wool Wash, and Yellowing.

XMAS

Decorations have always been an integral part of Christmas celebrations and nature's aromatic oils can be used very easily to add a natural and traditional touch to them.

Oranges studded with cloves are a classic Christmas decoration, with a delightful scent. Roll the studded oranges in clove or orange essential oils first, then roll them in a natural preservative such as orris root powder. Try a variation on the theme with different citrus fruits studded with cloves and rolled in their respective essential oils.

FRAGRANT PINE CONES

Pine cones, or any decorative seed pod, can be impregnated with oils such as pine and cedarwood, or with resins like frankincense and myrrh. Arrange in small baskets or hang and decorate with pieces of ribbon scented with essential oil. Add a drop of pine or cedarwood oil or some frankincense or myrrh resin to each cone or nut, plus 2 drops of essential oil on a cotton-wool ball and seal in a plastic bag for 24 hours.

AROMATIC WOOD

Interesting pieces of wood can also be impregnated with any of the Christmas oils to produce a long-lasting source of fragrance in your home. Scatter the scented wood along shelves, in drawers or use as a fragrant table arrangement.

Any pieces of dried wood or wood shavings can be used. Use your imagination to create something really different that will not only be visually impressive, but also aromatically satisfying.

Add the chosen essential oil to a container of water until well scented, then soak the wood. For a subtle 'Christmassy' colour you can add a few drops of an appropriate vegetable food dye. Suitable Christmas oils to use are cinnamon, clove, mandarin, orange, pine, cedarwood, and frankincense and myrrh resin.

OLD-FASHIONED CHRISTMAS WREATH

Make a garland from canes pruned from grape vines, wisteria or willow stems, or any other suitable vine, or purchase ready-made, twisted vine from a florist shop. Decorate your wreath by tucking in small bunches of herbs and sweetly scented flowers. Work in one direction around the circle — this will ensure that all the herbs travel in the same direction and overlap each other to conceal the stems. Hang immediately or leave to dry in a dark, dry place.

Use a combination of herbs and Australian natives. Ideal herbs to use as a background are rosemary and sage, which dry to an attractive silver-grey, or banksia, which will dry to a soft, pale fawn shade. Next, add herbs for colour: lavender will give your wreath splashes of lilac. Clove pinks are also an excellent choice. Calendulas and everlasting daisies will add a striking contrast. Other interesting additions can be pieces of cinnamon bark, or the pods and seeds of any unusual plant. Finish of with a loop of red or green satin ribbon to hang your wreath with.

FESTIVE TREATS

To make the festive season truly different, add essential oils derived from spices to your Christmas treats, such as cakes and desserts. Ginger oil in the Christmas pudding is a favourite in my household; it releases a heavenly aroma, as well as spicing up the pudding. Try any of the following spice oils in your cooking: cardamom, cinnamon, clove, mace, and nutmeg.

OVER-INDULGENCE

Regardless of our good intentions, it happens every Christmas. We swear that we won't over-indulge in all those tempting goodies, yet, somehow, most of us still succumb.

There is no way to miraculously dissolve away all that excess food, but we can use herbs and essential oils to relieve the associated discomfort. Better still, we can be realistic and prepare ourselves for the inevitable.

Camomile tea is excellent for calming down an overworked stomach; spearmint tea aids digestion and helps to dispel stomach gas. A mixture of equal parts peppermint, lemon balm and lemon verbena can be drunk after a heavy meal to aid digestion. Add 1 teaspoon of one of these dried herbs (or 1 teaspoon of a mixture of them) to a ceramic cup, pour in hot water, infuse for three minutes and strain. Adjust to taste with honey or lemon juice if preferred.

Another simple tea to aid digestion can be made using one of the following: lemon oil, ginger oil or peppermint oil. Put 1 or 2 drops of your chosen oil and a teaspoon of honey into a mug, pour in boiling water, stir until dissolved, and sip slowly.

Over-indulgence in alcohol leads to dehydration and results in those miserable sensations commonly called a hangover. To a greater or lesser degree, the body is having to cope with poisoning.

Beers and wines vary in their chemical content: some are classed as being organic — their ingredients were cultivated without chemicals, nor were chemicals added in their processing. Others, however, are almost chemical cocktails. Drinking good-quality organic beverages lessens the effects of hangovers in the short term and, in the longer term, will do less damage to your liver.

Other preventative measures against hangover include drinking plenty of water before you drink alcohol, or in between alcoholic drinks. This slows down the alcohol absorption rate and allows your body to cope better. Drink plenty of water after the party, as this will help to flush the toxins from your body. Before going to sleep, take around 1000 mg of vitamin C, but do not take any more than this (more than 1000 mg could cause diarrhoea). Avoid drinking black coffee, as this will only make things worse.

The best antidote for a hangover and indigestion, however, is moderation. Drink and eat sensibly, and your body will thank you.

See also Hangover.

YARROW FACE PACK

This is an excellent facial cleanser for oily skin.

*½ cup fresh (or ¼ cup dried)
yarrow leaves
100 g natural
yoghurt
1 tablespoon
finely ground
oatmeal
Distilled water*

Place the yarrow leaves in an enamel or stainless steel pan and add just enough distilled water to cover them. Cover the saucepan, bring to the boil and then reduce to a simmer for five minutes. Remove from heat, steep until cold, then strain through muslin.

Mix the yoghurt, oatmeal and 20 ml of the yarrow water to form a paste, adding more oatmeal if necessary, and spread over facial skin, but not around the eyes and mouth. Leave on for fifteen minutes, then rinse off with tepid water.

YEAST INFECTION

An effective natural remedy for yeast infection in women is to apply fresh, natural yoghurt inside the vagina one or two times daily. If symptoms persist, consult your health practitioner.

To treat yeast infections in babies and children, wash the affected area with garlic water, then gently apply garlic oil. Again, a health practitioner should be consulted if symptoms persist.

To make garlic water, chop 2 cloves of garlic and steep in 300 ml of hot water. Cool and strain.

To make garlic oil, chop up 6–12 cloves (depending on desired strength) and combine with 500 ml of sunflower oil in a tightly sealed glass jar. Allow to stand for fourteen days, then strain into an airtight glass bottle. Store in a dark, cool place.

YELLOWING

White knitted garments can become yellow and discoloured from exposure to direct sunlight, age or improper storage. If the problem is noticed in time, it may be possible to reverse the process.

Try soaking the garment for an hour in a bucket of warm water in which you have dissolved a cup of bicarbonate of soda. Then hand wash the garment in pure soap flakes and warm water. Rinse thoroughly in clean, warm water, wrap in a towel and wring out the excess water, then turn the garment inside-out and spread on a clean towel to dry, away from direct sunlight.

YOGHURT

You can make your own yoghurt at home using an inexpensive styrofoam cooler, or in a thermos flask. For either method, you will need to have a cooking thermometer.

STYROFOAM COOLER METHOD

Heat 1 litre of milk to 75°C. Pour 5 to 8 cm of water, which has been heated to 55°C, into the bottom of the cooler. Let the milk cool to 55°C and add a cup of commercial plain yoghurt, mix well, and pour into small containers with lids. Place the containers in the cooler, make sure the cooler lid is tightly secured and leave to stand for six to eight hours, at which time your yoghurt should be thick enough to take out and refrigerate.

Milk supplies vary, and this can affect the consistency of the yoghurt. If the batch is too thin, next time blend in 1 cup of instant powdered milk before adding the plain yoghurt.

Yoghurt can also be made in a styrofoam cooler using instant yoghurt culture (see Thermos Flask Method, below).

THERMOS FLASK METHOD

This method requires the purchase of a yoghurt culture, usually available from health-food stores.

Following the directions on the culture packet, mix the required amount with milk, heat to 45° to 55°C and pour into your thermos. Seal and leave for 3 to 4 hours. If it is not thick enough, leave it for a little while longer, then pour into containers and refrigerate.

ZINC

Zinc deficiency has been linked to both male and female infertility, susceptibility to infection, behavioural and sleep disturbances, white spots on nails and slow wound healing. Good natural sources are fish, lean meat, green leafy vegetables, pulses, nuts and wheatgerm. Zinc citrate in tablet form is also available.

Growing your own organic vegetables can be a big plus, as they contain more zinc than those grown with the help of chemical fertilisers. If it is not possible to grow your own, seek out a reliable supplier of organic produce.

Maintaining correct zinc levels in the body helps to decrease cholesterol deposits, preserves the sense of taste, helps to ensure fertility and, in men, keeps the prostate gland healthy.

ZUCCHINI

Zucchinis are a prolific-growing vegetable and you often end up with an over-abundance. Turn the excess into a delicious relish.

ZUCCHINI RELISH

4 cups minced zucchini
3 cups minced carrots
4½ cups minced onions
1½ cups minced capsicums
¼ cup organic salt
2¼ cups white vinegar
¾ cup sugar
1 tablespoon celery seed
¾ teaspoon dry mustard

Combine all ingredients in a large pan and cook for 20 minutes or until the vegetables are tender but not soft. While still hot, pack into hot sterilised bottling jars, seal, and process in a boiling water bath for 20 minutes.